i'm spiritual, dammit!

i'm Spiritual, dammit!

✳

how to
keep your feet
on the ground and
your head in the stars

JENNIFFER WEIGEL

HAMPTON ROADS
PUBLISHING COMPANY, INC.

Cover design by Laura Beers
Cover art © Digital Vision Illustration/Veer
Text design by Maxine Ressler
Typeset in Adobe Jenson Pro, Futura BT, and Ghetto Marquee

Hampton Roads Publishing Company, Inc.
Charlottesville, VA 22906
www.hrpub.com

Library of Congress Cataloging-in-Publication Data is available on request.

ISBN: 978-1-57174-634-4

10   9   8   7   6   5   4   3   2   1
Printed on acid-free paper in the United States of America
VG

contents

they walk among us

Embrace Your Gifts

A church sign from Lady of All
Saints Catholic Church reads:

The First Presbyterian Church across the
street countered that message by posting:

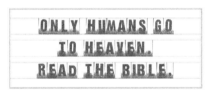

"You seem to be a magnet for really bizarre shit," my friend Steve
Cochran said during the commercial break of his radio show. He
was interviewing me for my first book, *Stay Tuned.*

"I like to think of it as being a gatherer of information concerning
paranormal or metaphysical circumstances that many consider to
be a coincidence," I said. "But *crazy shit* works too."

"You're like 'The *Medium* Whisperer,'" he said.

He was kind of right. Total strangers now felt safe sharing their
"I See Dead People" stories with me for some reason.

"So do you think it happens more often to you because you've done all these interviews with mediums and gurus? Or does it happen to *everyone*, and you're just more aware of it?" he asked.

"I think it's a little of both," I said.

"JENNY, IS that you?" the man said. I was standing on Michigan Avenue just *staring* at a person who looked vaguely familiar, hoping a lightbulb would go off.

College? No. . . . High school gym class? Nahh. . . . One night stand? Oh dear God!

"Yes?" I said, still not placing him.

"It's James," he said, like I knew only one James in the world.

James . . . James . . . James . . . J—oh, JAMES!

This wasn't just *any* James. This was the James who stopped me in my tracks in the fourth grade. The guy who made my stomach "flip" with a simple smile. The jock who was good at everything and dated the cheerleader. *That* James.

"Oh my GOD!" I yelled. "How are you?"

"Great! Jesus, it's been what, twenty years at least?"

We hadn't seen each other since high school, and now we were standing on the Magnificent Mile debating where we should catch up over a panini.

"So I HEAR you were a reporter on television?" he said, looking over the menu.

"Yeah. I quit that job after a few years, when I got sick of the negativity in the newsroom."

We filled each other in on the basics—he's married with two kids and lives on the East Coast. Works in technologies or some career with computers. I'm married with one kid, I explained, and live in the Chicago area. I mostly write these days.

"I was so sorry to hear about your dad," he said. "My parents sent me some articles when he died. He was so young."

"Fifty-six," I said.

"Didn't you write a book? I thought I remembered my parents saying something about that."

"Yeah."

"That is so amazing. You are an *author*," he gushed.

Everyone seems to think that once you write a book, you're either some sort of expert or you're rich.

Ha!

"There are days when I wonder if leaving my broadcasting gig was the right thing to do," I said. "I was making great money. Had health insurance. But I was miserable. I just hated reporting on tragedies and felt there was more out there for me, you know?"

"Yeah, I definitely get that," James said, taking a sip of his martini. "But things are going well for you now, right?"

"Of *course!*" I said. But that was only partially true. I was happy not working in the news business and doing my writing, but as a freelancer, I never knew where my next paycheck was coming from. I was getting tired of the panic that came with being self-employed.

"How did you get the courage to quit?" James asked.

I always struggle with this answer because it sounds so insane. "I sort of went on a quest and interviewed a bunch of mediums and psychics after my dad died, and I decided that life was too short to be miserable."

"Really?" James started chewing on one of his olives.

"Yeah. One of mediums was right here in Chicago, and she started telling me things that only my dad knew."

"And you believed her?" He was understandably skeptical.

"I never would have believed any of this if I hadn't experienced it for myself," I said. "I didn't give her my last name before I went in because I didn't want her to Google me, and she relayed an exact conversation that I had had with my dad when he was alive. Nobody was there for that conversation except myself and my dead father, so I don't know how she could have gotten the information."

James seemed interested. "You're a journalist. You probably know when you're being bullshitted, right?"

"I'd like to think so, yes."

We sat there for a moment. James ordered another drink. He was on his third, and we'd only been there for about forty-five minutes.

"I've met a lot of people who have *gifts* most people don't truly accept or understand," I said. "I'm just starting to think that maybe we don't have all the answers yet. So I keep asking questions."

Part of me felt like I was sixteen years old again, worried that the most popular boy at school wouldn't invite me to the keg party. What if James thought I'd totally lost my mind? But then I noticed something "click," as if it were now safe to share what he was about to say.

"You know, I don't really talk about this much, but I've had some experiences," he said.

"Experiences?"

"Well, for me, it's always been with colors. I see colors around people," he said, almost whispering.

"You mean auras?" I asked.

"Some people call it that, yeah. It's really helped me, especially in business."

Oh my God! The Homecoming King sees auras?!

He sipped his cocktail to see how I would react to what he was telling me.

"Go on," I smiled.

"If someone has brown or grey energy, I won't work with them," he said. "Purple, green, or yellow, then it's a done deal. My closest friends have violet energy."

James was very successful. Whatever he did with technologies had gotten him a very high title within his company.

"How long have you been able to see colors and energy?" I asked.

"Since I was about eight," he said, in a matter-of-fact tone.

No shit?!

"Everything is energy, so everything has a color. Even the trucks on the street," he said, pointing to a delivery van outside.

"That is so incredible. Do you know that people spend decades taking classes and meditating in hopes of being able to do what you can do naturally?"

I'd been *questing* myself for several years, interviewing every *woo-woo* author I could get my hands on—trying yoga, energy work, and intuition workshops. I'd been to drum circles, sweat lodges, spirituality conferences, even angel seminars. And after all that, I wasn't seeing any fucking colors, okay? I was just exhausted!

James took a big sip of his drink.

"I interviewed a psychic who drank a twelve pack a day," I said, trying to lighten the mood. "She told me it was to help quiet her gift because sometimes she didn't want to deal with it."

James let out a nervous laugh. He could sense my concern with his mid-day boozing.

"I'm finding out that there are a lot more people out there like you than you'd think," I said, trying to let him know that this "seeing energy stuff" was not a curse. "It's an incredible thing to be able to do what you do."

James just stared at me. I wondered what he saw.

"Do you see any colors around *me?*" I asked.

"Yes. You've got yellow coming from all sides," he said without hesitation, as if he was giving me the weather forecast.

Yellow? Is that good?

"But there's a slight sadness in your eyes," he said. "They're grey."

I started to panic that James could read my thoughts, too. If he could see auras, then maybe he could sense that I was scared about my career? I did my best to look away and not make eye contact. Feeling my discomfort, he quickly changed the subject.

"When you were on stage in high school, you were bright yellow and violet," he said.

"You saw me in plays?" I was afraid I was going to start blushing. While I had been in all the school productions, I didn't think a jock like James took notice.

"Of course," he said. "You are a natural. Do you ever think about getting back into it?"

Funny he should bring that up. I had just been talking to one of my girlfriends about turning my first book into a one-woman show. It had always been a dream of mine. "I've thought about it, yeah."

"You should do it. When I mentioned it just now, you lit up. Literally," he laughed.

Oh shit! Now he can see me light up?!

"You know, that medium I was talking about who supposedly saw my dad? Well, she says being intuitive is like playing the piano—everyone has the ability to strike a key, but some can only play chopsticks and other people are Mozart. It's different levels, but everyone has it." I felt like I'd been stuck in "chopsticks" mode for a while now, and here I was sitting with Mozart.

James nodded, but my words didn't seem to ease his mind.

"What does your wife think of your ability to see colors?" I asked.

"We don't talk about it," he said.

I started to understand a bit more why he might have been drinking so much.

After lunch, we went our separate ways. We vowed to keep in touch, but I knew that probably wasn't going to happen.

"I'm going to write about you," I said, as we waved goodbye.

"Okay," he said. "Just be sure to change my name...."

THE FOLLOWING week, I was walking with my son Britt, when he got sidetracked by the firemen washing their trucks in the street.

"Mommy, can we see the fiyah twucks?" he blurted out. It was a hot summer day, and he was entranced by the flurry of activity.

"Are you a junior firefighter, little guy?" one of the firemen asked. He was holding a plastic fire hat that he handed to Britt. Thus a love affair between my toddler and loud, shiny red trucks was born.

"Whoa!" Britt said, as they let him ring the bell.

"You look familiar," a man with the nametag *Danny* said, approaching me.

"Really?"

After a little small talk, we discovered that Danny used to watch me when I was a reporter for CBS.

"I think you and my mother were our only viewers," I joked.

Danny laughed. "So what are you up to now if you're not on CBS anymore?"

"Well, I wrote a book, and I do talks."

"What's the book about?"

I hesitated, trying to think of a description that didn't seem too weird. "I left my cushy broadcasting job to *find myself*, and then traveled the country to try to talk to my dead dad through mediums and psychics," I said, waiting for a reaction along the lines of "Oh, so you're *nuts?!*"

Danny leaned in to talk to me, as if he didn't want the other firemen to hear him. "Step into my office for a second, won't you, Jenniffer?"

I looked back at Britt. He was sitting in fireman Joe's lap pretending to steer the big rig, happy as a clam.

"I've got him," Joe said, as I looked over.

Danny closed the door.

"I've had angels whispering in my ear since I was about six," he said in a matter-of-fact tone.

I looked into the fireman's eyes. He seemed very sincere. He had a sweet face and a rock-solid frame that could probably lift a car if he put his mind to it.

"Angels?" I asked. "What kind of stuff are they whispering?"

"All sorts of things. From 'turn left at the light' to 'call in sick today.' I hear them loud and clear."

Danny went on to explain that he'd been guided by what he called the *voices of angels* since his childhood, and the voices have never steered him wrong. They've even saved his life on several occasions.

"I also see spirits," he said, in an intense whisper. "My one buddy that died in a fire walks around here all the time, giving me shit." He laughed. "He moves our equipment around and flickers the lights. But I can't say a damn thing to any of these guys around here because they'd think I'd lost my fucking mind!"

But you can tell me . . .

"I'm going to bring you a copy of my book, Danny," I said. "I think you'll enjoy some of the stories in there."

We exchanged emails as I tried to peel Britt off one of the engines.

"No home!" Britt yelled, as if I were putting hot pokers in his eyes. "NO HOME!"

A few days later, I dropped off a book for Danny; within two days, he had read the entire thing. We became email friends, sharing stories of "coincidences." I brought Britt back to the station, and our conversations continued.

"So tell me about this Therese lady," he asked, referring to one of the mediums from the book. Therese Rowley is a Catholic CEO consultant, with a master's degree and a PhD in business, who also happens to read energy and see dead people. I call her the ultimate "combo platter."

"She's a genuine Catholic, huh?" Danny asked. He, too, was Catholic, and he was concerned that his talk of mediums might mean he wouldn't be let through the Pearly Gates.

"She is very Catholic, yes," I said. "Goes to Mass. Almost every day, actually. One of eleven children. Been able to see spirits since she was a very young girl. Kept it secret for years because she's Catholic. I think you should meet her for sure, Danny. She'd love to hear your stories. You two have a lot in common."

Eventually, I sent Therese an email mentioning my new fireman friend, and she quickly wrote him a note asking to meet for lunch. Could you imagine being a fly on the wall for *that* conversation? Two practicing Catholics who see dead people?!

A few weeks went by, and I didn't hear from Danny. I asked Therese if they met for lunch, and she told me that they had set up a meeting, but he cancelled. I sent an email to Danny, and after a few days of silence, I finally got a response:

"I don't think I should be meeting any mediums. My priest says that it's the work of the devil, and I surely don't want to mess with that."

I never heard from him again.

"Isn't the Bible *all* about talking to dead people?" I asked Therese one night as we were chatting on the phone. I was so disappointed that Danny had gotten too scared to even have a sandwich with her.

At that moment, I heard my son making noises through the baby monitor.

"Hey, Therese, I've gotta go. Sounds like my son is still up," I said, as I headed upstairs. When I entered his room, Britt was rolling on his bed, looking at the ceiling, laughing at nothing.

"Who are you talking to, honey?"

He pointed to the ceiling. "The guy."

"What guy?"

"Right there!" he said, pointing again at the air.

"Well, what's he doing?"

"He's giving me a fiyah truck," he laughed.

"Oh really? That sure is nice. You can play with your fire truck in the morning."

I closed the door and heard laughing for a few more minutes. Eventually, he trailed off to sleep.

The next day, Britt and I were playing in the basement when his ball went under my husband's desk. He stopped at the desk and pointed at a picture of my dad from my wedding day.

"There's the guy, Momma," he said.

"What guy?"

"Who gave me the fiyah truck," he said with a smile.

I almost fell over. "That's the guy who was in your room?"

"Uh-huh," he nodded.

So apparently, even dead grandparents can shower their grandkids with presents.

"That is your grandpa, sweetie," I said, trying not to cry.

"My gwampa?"

"Yes. Mommy's dad. He is an angel now up in Heaven."

As the weeks went by, I struggled with how I was going to share these stories with my husband Clay. He had been supportive when I went on my journey to interview mediums for my first book, but I was worried he'd think I was going to run off and join a cult if I told him I thought our son could see dead people.

But Britt's late-night chats kept coming . . .

"Stop it!" I heard Britt say through the baby monitor a few weeks later. He was laughing.

I walked in, and he was squirming around as if he was being tickled.

"What on earth is going on here, cutie?" I said, sitting on his bed.

"It's Gwampa!" he said, with a smile.

"Your grandpa is here? What's he doing?"

"He's smacking my butt," he said, rolling to his side as he pointed to his fanny.

My jaw dropped.

My father had a thing for whacking people in the ass. Especially with his wives and his kids. It was his answer for everything—from affection to annoyance. Whether I was five or twenty-five, I could always count on my dad coming up from behind and hitting my tush with great gusto, while chanting: *must-be-jelly-cuz-jam-don't-shake-like-that* [pause] *BABY!* (He would use particular force and volume for "BABY!")

This was really embarrassing at my college graduation, by the way.

"How is Grandpa smacking your butt?" I asked.

Britt pushed me off the bed and stood behind me.

"Like this, Momma."

He then took his right hand and proceeded to smack my rear end *Weigel style.*

As his cute little fingers patted my buns, I tried to think how this could be possible. Britt was only a toddler. Even if he had heard Mommy and Daddy talking about the way Grandpa used to "whack our asses," would he really be savvy enough to hold on to that information and then use it down the road as he's drifting off to sleep?

How come he can see you and I can't, Dad?

Perhaps Britt overheard a story when my uncle Tony was in town? Maybe he was just intuitive and picking up on my sadness that Grandpa wasn't around to take advantage of his grandson's precious little booty?

I went to my computer and composed a blog post on the subject before heading to bed.

When I woke up the next day, the responses from readers started coming in like wildfire. Parent after parent shared their children's "conversations with dead people." From secret nicknames being voiced by unknowing three-year-olds, to first graders finding lost pieces of jewelry on command from a dead aunt, the stories were extraordinary.

"Our two-and-a-half-year-old daughter knew the day her grandmother died," one woman wrote. "Before we even told her, she looked up at us from her crib and said 'Grandma is with the angels now. She just told me how beautiful it is in her new house.'"

I started to think about fireman Danny and James—men who have an ability that they're ashamed to talk about. I wondered how many other people might be walking among us who are struggling with gifts they aren't encouraged to nurture. And how different their lives would have been if this behavior were considered "normal."

THE NEXT time I tucked Britt into bed, I decided to tell him that whatever he saw, was okay with me. "A lot of kids can see angels, sweetie," I said, as I tickled his back. "Even some grown-ups."

"You?" Britt asked, as he sucked on his fingers.

I wish!

"No, honey. But next time Grandpa comes, you can tell him Mommy says 'hi,'" I joked.

"Mmmm hmmmm," he said, as he drifted off to sleep.

the power of one

You Are Where You're Supposed to Be in Every Moment

Lady of All Saints Catholic Church
posted a response to the First Presbyterian Church across the street:

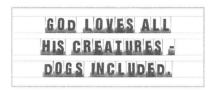

GOD LOVES ALL
HIS CREATURES -
DOGS INCLUDED.

"HEY JEN, it's Rafe!" My brother said on the other end of the phone.

Rafer had just been hired as the sportscaster for HLN to be on *Morning Express* with Robin Meade. It was a snowy night in December 2007, and I was on my way to a book signing in Park Ridge.

"I just signed the contract!" he yelled. "It's a done deal. I'm so psyched! We're about to pop the champagne."

"That's great," I said, trying to feign excitement.

"What are *you* up to?"

Not only was I lost, but now it was snowing sideways. "Oh, just trying to find Burke's Books for another book signing," I said, looking around for a street sign. "Don't you wish you could trade places with *me* right about now?"

"You gonna have a big crowd tonight?"

My book had been out for a couple months, and I'd already called in every favor from every friend and family member for the initial launch. On this cold winter night in the middle of the week, I hadn't invited a single soul.

"I kinda doubt it," I sighed.

"Okay, well have fun, and I'll talk to you later!" Rafer said.

I threw the phone down on my passenger seat and started feeling sorry for myself.

If I hadn't quit my job at CBS, maybe I'd be working at CNN now! Rafer is sipping bubbly, and I'm lost in Park Ridge driving in a fucking snowstorm!

Not even a few seconds later, the phone rang again. "Hello!" I yelled, putting the phone on speaker.

"Hey Jen, it's Therese Rowley," the voice said. "What are you up to?"

I took a deep breath and exploded. "Tell me I made the right decision by leaving my job in television?! I'm driving around in circles and can't find this bookstore. I have no idea where I'm going, and Rafer just got hired by Headline News!"

I fought back tears as Therese tried to douse the flames. "Okay, first of all, I want you to pull over. You should not be driving in this condition," she said in a calming voice. "Pull over right now."

I pulled off to the side of the road and put the car in "park."

"I'll be fine. I'm just feeling sorry for myself," I said.

"Every single one of us has a unique journey," said Therese. "You and Rafer are on totally different paths. You can't compare yourself to him or to anyone else out there. You are touching people every day with your book, and you don't even know it. Just because you don't have a television job with ratings to tell you how many people are tuning in, doesn't mean that you're not 'tuning in' to the Universe's master plan for you."

I watched as the snowflakes fell onto the windshield. Having turned off my wipers, they were starting to block my entire view. I didn't care.

"You have to remember—*you are where you're supposed to be in every moment.* Truly. Even if you just reach one person tonight. It may be the owner of the store or a person shopping in the store. That one person will be changed by you, and that's just as important as if you were speaking to millions of people on CNN."

I tried to soak in what Therese was saying. I had been raised in a media family where your success was measured by the status of your career. When I was growing up, every conversation at the dinner table involved listing accomplishments. If you didn't have something magnificent to throw into the ring, you were criticized. I had a hard time thinking that a talk for *one person* in Park Ridge could be considered a "success."

"The gardener is just as important as Angelina Jolie or Oprah," Therese continued. "Only the human ego thinks one is more important than the other."

I took a deep breath. "Okay," I said.

"I like to call it 'perfect timing and divine order.' Everything happens in the order it's supposed to," she said. "Say this after me—*you are where you're supposed to be at every moment.*"

"You are where you're supposed to be at every moment," I growled.

"Now go have fun, and let me know how it goes," she said.

I hung up the phone and picked up my directions. I looked up. My windshield view was now barely existent. I tried to find a locator; a store sign maybe. I looked out to see where I was parked.

I was pulled over in a legal parking space right in front of Burke's Books.

Damn that Therese is good.

I gathered my things and walked through the front door. As I entered the store, I saw about thirty empty chairs set up along with a table, and a poster-sized sign of my book on display.

"Hi there!" A woman behind the counter said to me. "Are you Jenniffer?"

"Yes," I said. I looked down at my watch. It was 7:00 p.m. on the dot. My talk was supposed to start right at 7:00, and there was no one in sight.

"I'm Pat Willoughby. I own the store," she said, looking at the empty room. "You invited people to come, right?" She seemed worried.

"Of *course.*" I lied. "Maybe the weather is keeping them away?"

I walked over to the corner of the room and leaned against the bookshelves as I called home. I pulled my huge winter coat up over my head so I could whimper in private, but the answering machine picked up.

"Please pick up. Please pick up, Clay. There's *nobody* here! *Nobody!* If you can hear this, drag Britt out of his bed and please come to Park Ridge. I am *such* a *loser!*"

My voice squeaked off into nothingness as I listened to silence on the other end of the phone. I hung up in defeat, lowered my coat, took a deep breath, and turned around to face the music.

Okay, Jen. You can do this. So, nobody is here. Who cares?

I walked over to the table and sat down.

You are not a loser. You are where you're supposed to be in every moment.

I tried to believe the mantra running through my mind as I arranged the books on the table, pretending to look busy. Suddenly, I heard the front door open. Both Pat and I snapped to attention to see who was coming. To our relief, it was a group of women.

"Welcome!" Pat said with a smile. I looked closely at the group. I knew none of them, but they were indeed there to see me.

Phew!

Slowly but surely, people started trickling in. Within about fifteen minutes, I had more than twenty strangers sitting in the seats, waiting to hear me talk. It wasn't a full stadium, but it was definitely better than an empty room.

I looked around and saw a sweet, young girl sitting in the back row. She looked like she was in her early twenties. There was a sadness in her eyes that really struck me. I started to wonder if she too had lost someone close to her.

I led my talk with the story of what had *just* happened to me: "You are where you're supposed to be in every moment," I explained. I was wondering about my choices and then magically found myself in front of the store that I had been unable to find in the storm. I talked about meeting James Van Praagh twice and traveling to a small town in New York named Lily Dale where a community of mediums, psychics, and healers has lived since the late 1800s.

After the talk, while I was signing books, the young woman who had caught my eye approached the table.

"Thanks so much for this," she said, handing me her book to sign.

"What's your name?" I asked.

"Katie. I wasn't going to come tonight, but I'm really glad I did. I needed a good laugh," she said.

As I was signing her book, I got this strange feeling that I needed to give her my personal email address. "Here is my email," I said. "I want to know what you think of the book."

"Okay," she said, slightly surprised.

As she walked away, Pat came up to the table.

"Wow, I haven't seen Katie smile in months," she said.

"What happened to her?"

"Her dad was shot and killed last year—in her driveway one morning after he'd just had breakfast with the family. He was the best guy. So loved by everyone. It was devastating."

I thought losing my dad to a brain tumor was tragic, but I couldn't imagine having breakfast with Dad one minute and have him murdered in the driveway the next.

"They still don't know who did it or why," Pat explained. "Katie's a schoolteacher. She and her father were very close. She's having a hard time with the loss."

"I hope she keeps in touch," I said.

A COUPLE OF months later, I was looking through my emails, and I saw one from Katie:

> After I read your book, I no longer felt like my dad was out of reach. I just had to "listen" for him. That really touched me, and as soon as I started to think that way, I started noticing things. I finished your book when I was on vacation in Arizona. We went on a tour and the guide asked me what my name was, and I said "Katie," and he said "Can I call you my little Kate?" I just about fell over because that was my dad's nickname for me; *my little Kate*. It was as if time stood still, and I just stared at this guide, knowing it was a "wink" from my dad. Now if I have a particularly hard day, I will ask my dad for help and guidance. Many times now, when I focus on the cars in front of me, there will be my dad's navy Blazer leading the way.

Within weeks, Katie found herself making an appointment with medium Therese Rowley. I was amazed when Katie shared all the details.

> At first I was really skeptical. And then my dad came bursting through. He described the family room and said that going to the 'Other Side' was like stepping off the elliptical machine. We have one of those in our family room, and he said that life is like the elliptical machine; you're exercising and watching TV, and when this life ends, you just step off the machine. You are still here but in a different way. He said that he can help me so much more from where he is now than if

he had breakfast with me every morning. I asked Therese about the man who shot my dad and she said my father was working with him from the Other Side. My father's killer was a young man who'd had an abusive childhood, so he didn't value other lives. My dad said it didn't matter if this young man was caught, because he would still try to help him love himself more. Dad was a coach and always worked with the kid who was having the hardest time. That is just what he would have said.

So even if you are gunned down in your driveway, you are where you're supposed to be in every moment?

Katie continued with her story.

He showed Therese a blanket that he said was a gift from me (which it was), and he said that I should just put that blanket around me as if he was hugging me. I just knew Therese was for real. She couldn't have known about that blanket that I gave him. Or what our family room looked like. I just feel so much better knowing that he's looking out for me. He says that he is always going to be looking out for me.

Of course Katie would rather have her dad here with her every day, sharing breakfast at the kitchen table, but she's been given some relief by just thinking that maybe he really is closer than she thought.

"He says he will always protect me," she said. "I just know he is watching over me."

I called Therese to let her know that Katie benefited from her session.

"You were supposed to go to that bookstore so you could meet Katie," Therese said. "*You are where you're supposed to be in every moment. There really is no such thing as death* because nobody dies, you just change forms," she added. "If we could all wrap our heads around that reality, we'd be in a much better place with all of this, don't you think?"

I remembered the words of James Van Praagh when I interviewed him several years earlier: "The living have a lot harder time with dying than the dead. It's as if they're in the next room."

THE FOLLOWING month, I was doing a talk for about three hundred women, and I told the story about Katie. Afterwards, I was signing books, and a woman came up to me and said, "I know Katie and her family. My son dated Katie during the time when her father was killed."

It took me a moment to realize how wild this was; we were at least sixty miles from the Chicago area, and a woman in the crowd knew one of the people I mentioned in my talk?

"I will tell her you said 'hi'!" I said. I was not in constant contact with Katie, but this woman's mention of her made me feel the need to email her when I got home.

When I logged on to my computer that night, I was amazed to find that Katie had beaten me to the punch and sent me an email. She said that she had been to visit her grandmother on her father's side, and the *coincidences* continued.

> I told my grandma about meeting you and reading your book. She smiled and walked over to a drawer. She pulled out a picture of my dad when he was about twenty-three, getting an autograph from *your* dad at one of his appearances. I couldn't believe my grandma pulled out that picture of both of our dads right after I finished talking about you.

So apparently my dad and Katie's dad are buddies in Heaven.

WHEN IT came time to promote my book on the West Coast, the first stop was San Diego. I had been there several times to meet with my literary agent Bill Gladstone, and now I had been asked to speak at a conference called "101 Powerful Women . . . and a Few Good Men."

"You'll talk for about twenty minutes, and then we'll put your books on a table so you can sell them afterwards," said Bettie, the author who was in charge of the conference.

I had invited Therese to come along so I had some company. She was in the process of getting her own book together and was going to be meeting with Bill to discuss the details. It was a great excuse for us to work and play at the same time.

I started off the morning by doing an interview with one of the local television stations.

"Sit here Miss Wee-gal, and you'll be taken onto the set as we get closer to your segment," a woman said, as she placed me in the greenroom. It was really funny to be on the other end of this interview process. For years, I was the morning show person trying to bullshit my way through a conversation with an author. Now I was sitting in a greenroom with seven circus performers who were waiting to do backflips and ride a unicycle on the set of *Good Morning San Diego*.

*I left my six-figure salary for **this**?*

Within minutes, I was brought onto a set where the anchorman and one of the female anchors were seated.

"So Jenniffer, tell me about your book," the anchorman said, looking through his notes.

I quickly realized that he hadn't even opened my book, which was fine. I'd been in his shoes before, so I tried to make it easy on him.

"In a nutshell: I quit my job in the media to interview some spiritual gurus, mediums, and psychics and then wrote a humorous memoir about it," I said.

"Whoa," the anchorwoman said. "You quit your media job in *Chicago?*"

The man's eyes widened. It seemed that the subject matter piqued his interest.

"I think there's something to this stuff," he said.

"You do?" The anchorwoman said.

"Yes," he continued. "I didn't used to, but when I worked at a station in Indiana, the cops tipped us off to a psychic who helped with a lot of missing persons cases. So my cameraman and I went to interview her about a story I was working on . . ."

He started to lean into the table as his tone got serious. "She was this sweet old lady with white hair. But when we got back to the station and popped in the tapes to watch them, the woman wasn't the same person we had interviewed . . ."

Huh?!

"It was this old Native American woman. I swear to God; the cameraman and I just sat there rubbing our eyes. We interviewed one person, and here was a totally different person on the tape. It was the craziest thing I've ever seen. I mean, that's impossible, right?" he asked, almost looking for validation.

At this point, the anchorwoman looked like she had seen a ghost. This was not their typical "pre-interview" conversation.

"I was so freaked out that I locked the tapes up in a closet and never looked at them again. I haven't spoken about it since."

The anchorwoman tried to compose herself as the floor director approached.

"Here we go guys, we're back in 5 - 4 - 3 . . ."

THAT AFTERNOON, Therese and I headed to the conference. As we sat at a table waiting for the keynote speakers to begin, I noticed that Therese was squinting.

"What's the matter?" I asked.

She pointed to the elderly couple sitting in front of us. "Man, there is so much light coming from these two. It's like they are both *angels* or something!"

Her excitement level was equal to, say, having a giant celebrity in the room.

Oh my GOD! Brad Pitt!

Therese sort of shook her head back and forth, and started to exhale. I looked around to make sure nobody was staring. She did this sort of "puffing and exhaling" thing whenever she tapped into someone's energy. Perfectly fine when you're in a session, but sort of unsettling if you don't know what it means or you're around lots of strangers in public.

"Are you okay?" I whispered. Therese never talked about her gifts. If anything, she kept them very quiet, because she hails from a huge Catholic family. But every once in a while, she'd forget that the rest of the world *can't* see beams of light coming from someone's head.

"Don't you feel that?" she asked, still squinting.

Uh . . . Nope.

"I've got to find out who they are," Therese said.

At that moment, someone got on stage to announce the keynote speaker; Millard Fuller. Millard was the founder of Habitat for Humanity and the Fuller Center for Housing. He and his wife were the glowing couple sitting right in front of Therese.

Therese continued to exhale deeply as he got up from his chair. He gracefully walked to the podium and faced the crowd. Millard was tall and majestic, and as he shared his story of faith, I was totally entranced. His entire life was dedicated to building homes for those who needed them. Whenever he was struggling along his journey, he would magically be guided to a person who would help his cause. He said it was God who led the way.

"I gave it up to the Lord, and he always showed me the right path," he said.

I've always been turned off by the overly religious. In my experience, they usually come off as judgmental or superior. I had several people who refused to read my first book because they claim it encouraged the "Devil's Work" by talking about mediums or psychics. But Millard's faith was just the opposite. He didn't jam it down our throats. He was simply sharing how it drove him to serve. His never-ending faith got him out of bed, sustained his hard-charging work day, and assured him a good night's rest. I was so envious of his complete trust in God's presence. His energy was so nurturing I wanted to kidnap Millard Fuller and take him home with me.

"He's like a guardian angel," I said to Therese.

"No wonder he's beaming," she said.

AFTER THE lunch break, it was time for the other speakers. I looked at the list, which contained at least fifty people.

"Jesus, is this conference going until midnight?" I whispered.

I sat there trying to do the math in my head and quickly realized they'd overbooked the speakers. There was no way in hell all of us were going to get to talk for five minutes, let alone twenty.

I saw the panic start to build in the organizer's eyes as each speaker approached the stage. Slowly but surely, she shortened their time. First to fifteen minutes, then ten minutes, then five minutes.

When it got to be my turn, a woman grabbed my arm as I approached the stage, and whispered, "Keep it to three minutes, honey."

THREE MINUTES?! I flew all the way to San Diego for three fucking minutes?!

I looked out at the huge crowd and started to panic. I saw Millard Fuller. He had just moved the entire room to tears, and I now had 180 seconds to try and muster one coherent thought.

When I reached the podium, I drew a blank. Eventually, I formed some words, but I have no idea what came out of my mouth. It didn't feel very enlightening. As I got off the stage, I blew right past my table and headed for the bathroom. I made a beeline for the last stall, closed the door, and sat on the toilet.

I sucked. I can't believe I just blew it in front of so many people.

As I grabbed some tissue paper to wipe my eyes, I heard someone come in to the bathroom. I followed the "clip-clop" of the heels walking up and down the rows. They stopped in front of my stall.

"Is that Jenniffer Weigel?" a voice said.

Can't a person cry in the crapper in peace?

I tried to compose myself enough to answer. "Who wants to know?" I asked, wiping my nose.

"My name is Barbara. I saw you on *Good Morning San Diego* today. I never come to these conferences, but I just had to share a story with you."

I blew my nose and opened the stall.

At least ONE person was listening.

"Wow, that is so sweet," I said.

She stuck out her hand to introduce herself.

"Let me wash my hands really quick," I said.

"What you said about keeping your eyes out for the signs and signals from our loved ones who have died, that just really stuck for me," she said. "My dad recently died, and I have been really upset about it lately. I never ever watch *Good Morning San Diego*. Nothing against the show, I just don't usually have time in the mornings, but something told me to turn it on just as your interview was starting," she explained, barely coming up for air. "After the show, I went into the office, and a little bird followed me into the building. We've never had a bird fly into our office building before, but there it was, sitting right at my cubical as I got my things. When I was leaving, I tried to catch it, and it didn't even struggle. It just let me hold it in my hands. I walked outside with this little bird, and as I opened my hand to let it fly away, it just sat perched on my finger. It was just staring at me. It wouldn't move!"

The woman was now about two inches from my nose. I could practically taste what she had for breakfast, but I didn't dare interrupt. She was on a roll.

"The thing is, my dad was a huge bird watcher. He was always studying them and pointing out different types to me. It was his *thing*. This was a little songbird, one of Dad's favorites. I just know it was my dad. I never would have even *thought* that if I hadn't watched your interview this morning. I would have just thought it was strange that a bird flew into work, and that would have been the end of it." Her eyes started to well up. "Thank you, Jenniffer Weigel, for opening my mind up to receive that little message."

When I got back to my seat, I shared the encounter with Therese.

"You see. All it takes is one. You have no idea how this will change her journey. *You are where you're supposed to be in every moment,*" she said.

THAT NIGHT, my book agent had organized a large group for dinner that included the Fullers. The main purpose of the gathering was to talk about converting Millard's life story into a movie. There was a director, a writer, and some possible investors. The hope was that through all of our varied contacts, we could connect the dots enough to bring this project to life.

Everyone was having a nice time; however, I noticed that Millard's wife seemed uneasy. It turned out she was having issues with the possibility of being thrust into the limelight if this movie became a reality. Millard shared that it was most important to feature his faith in God as the main focus of the movie.

"Without God, I would not be here," he said.

I saw the writer roll his eyes. This was a Hollywood guy and not a church fan by any means. He did not want to be told how to write a movie script, but he listened to Millard's concerns. The director also chimed in, and the conversation started to get a bit heated. The writer was worried that too much talk of religion would turn off the "non-Christian" movie fans. Millard was insistent that God be the star and not Millard.

Millard's wife spoke of her worries about being in the public eye. Turns out, in Millard's younger days, he strayed from his marriage. Through faith and determination, however, the Fullers stayed together.

I hadn't said much the entire dinner, but I felt compelled to interject.

"Oh wow, Millard, I am so relieved to hear that you're actually human!" I blurted out. Millard looked at me and let out a genuine howl. His wife smiled.

"You and your wife are an inspiration. In my family, my parents got remarried every seven years," I said. "I think if you focus the storyline on your relationship, really expanding on the love you share through good times and bad, that will be an award-winning movie."

As we were leaving the restaurant a couple hours later, Millard came over to say good-bye.

"I sure hope some of your *faith* and *trust* will rub off on me," I said.

"Young lady . . . I've decided that I really like you," Millard said with a smile.

"I've decided that I really like you too, Millard."

I handed him a copy of my book. "No pressure to read it, Millard, but I want you to have this," I said.

"Is it signed?"

"Of course!"

"Good," he smiled.

He put out his arms and hugged me tight.

AFTER I got home from California, the phone rang. It was my mother. "Did you have a huge crowd and wow the West Coast?"

"The trip was incredible," I said. "My speech didn't turn out exactly like I'd hoped, but the people I talked to seemed touched."

"Oh that's wonderful, honey," she said.

I chuckled, remembering the woman who followed me into the bathroom. "I was exactly where I was supposed to be. I'm so glad I went."

Later that day, I was surprised to see an email from Millard waiting for me in my inbox.

Dear Jenniffer,

My goodness, what a treat it was to meet you and to be with you and so many other fine people at the conference this past Friday. You really made a big impression on me. You are quite an extraordinary person.

Thanks also, Jenniffer, for giving me a copy of your new book. I have already started reading it and have found it to be so well written. I am sure it is going to be a success in the marketplace.

If you are ever traveling down this way, Jenniffer, I hope you will come by for a visit. Please know that you will find a warm welcome awaiting you.

I send best regards.

Sincerely,
Millard Fuller

judgments, a rat, and big dicks

Don't Take It Personally

First Presbyterian Church responded
to The Lady of All Saints by posting:

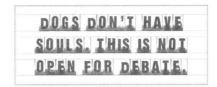

"I'm on the big slide!" Britt said with pride as we played at the park.

My son didn't really start talking until the day he turned three. He went from being mute to not being able to shut up. While he has become quite the "Chatty Cathy," he isn't very clear with some of his consonants. His "S" sounds like a "D" and his "R" a "W." For the most part, I can make out what he's saying with a little patience. He also gets his needle stuck if he wants things a certain way, and will repeat things one hundred times in hopes of getting his point across.

"I don't wanna go, Mom," he said with a sigh.

Leaving Britt's favorite "fire truck" park was always difficult, especially because he'd found a stick that he wanted to take home. Since we already had a collection of sticks a mile long in the backyard, I nixed the idea and went to put him in the car seat.

That's when the fun began.

"No, Momma. I want my big dick!"

Obviously, I knew what he meant, but he screamed this at the top of his lungs as I was trying to buckle him in, so we were quite the spectacle with the park crowd.

"Mommy, where's my dick? Give me my big dick! I want my big dick! Now!"

I started to get the giggles so bad that I almost couldn't latch his belt. I looked over my shoulder, hoping that nobody else had heard, and I made eye contact with a woman who gave me an evil glare. She was covering her three-year-old's ears and shaking her head in disapproval.

First of all, I wanted to tell this chick to get laid or get bent for not having a better sense of humor. Who were we *really* disturbing? So her little girl heard the word "dick"; I doubt she knows what that is. (And if she does, then her mom shouldn't be judging me!)

I thought about walking up to her and getting in her grill with a "who do you think you are giving me the look of death" speech.

Then I thought of don Miguel Ruiz.

Don't take it personally.

I had interviewed don Miguel Ruiz several years before, and it truly changed my life. He was coming through Chicago, promoting the paperback release of his bestselling book, *The Four Agreements*. The one agreement that always seems to pop up in my life is "don't take it personally."

"Someone's reaction to you has nothing to do with you," he told me. "If you are doing your best and embracing a spiritual practice, it's not about you. We have no idea what is going on inside someone's mind or body."

As I became a mother, this philosophy really hit me on a new level.

"We all want to control our kids or even our parents," don Miguel said. "We are each responsible for our own lives and nobody else's. It's as if we are making a movie, and we need to write it, cast it, and direct it. The people in our lives are just actors playing a role. Only *you* can decide what happens in your life story."

Now that I was a mother of a three-year-old, I had a hard time accepting that I'm just the hired gun to play Britt's mom. (I'd like Jennifer Garner to be me in the film version, by the way . . .) I wanted to make sure Britt was safe at all times and help him make good choices. Was that so wrong?

"All we can do is lead by example. Those around us will watch how you live your life, and hopefully, they will want to emulate that behavior," don Miguel told me.

If I yelled at this lady at the park, It probably wouldn't be a shining example of behavior for my son to "emulate."

Don't take it personally.

Maybe this woman hadn't seen a "big dick" in a long time and she was feeling bitter. Maybe her dog just died.

Or maybe she's just a primo North-shore bitch.

Whatever the reason, it wasn't something I wanted to take on. I hurried into my car with my very pissed-off three-year-old gaining momentum and started to drive away.

"My BIG DICK! Mommy, where is my big dick? GIVE ME MY BIG DICK! MMYYYY DICK!"

I know this is such potty humor, but hey, when you have a miniature person saying very adult words at full volume, it's pretty darn hilarious.

I called my husband Clay to tell him of our whereabouts, but he didn't pick up the phone. I did my best to leave a message.

"We're leaving the park now.... *GIVE ME MY DICK!* Um, Britt's a little upset ... *MY BIG DICK! MY DICK!*"

We made it home, but I don't think Britt took a breath for the whole seven-minute drive. I tried to count the number of times he said "dick," but I stopped keeping track after twenty-seven.

When he got to our backyard and started playing with other "dicks," he soon forgot about the one from the park.

But hours later, when I was reading him a story after his bath, he looked into my eyes and reminded me with a whisper that he remembered everything.

"Mommy, tomorrow can we go and get my big dick. *Tweeeease?*"

How could I say no to that? He said *"tweeeease."*

THE NEXT night, I had a book talk downtown, and, for some reason, I was a little nervous.

"Why are you nervous?" Clay asked.

"I haven't done one in a while," I said.

There were about forty people at this talk when I arrived. They seated me at one end of the room and asked me to speak for forty-five minutes or so. Afterwards, there would be a Q-and-A session. As I got settled onto my stool, I started telling stories from the book and noticed a woman in the front row. She had her arms crossed and a terrible scowl on her face.

"Bestselling author James Van Praagh told me that there really is no such thing as Hell but that Hell is here on earth," I said.

"Yeah right!" the woman blurted out.

I was sort of taken aback by her comment, but I continued. "He says that our afterlife experience reflects the way we were on earth, so if you were a mass murderer, you are not going to be hanging out with the Saints like my grandma Ginny," I said. "But he says you do have a sort of 'life review,' where you literally see and feel every emotion you ever put out. It's like reliving your life in an instant. So depending on how you treated others, this can be heaven, or this can be hell."

"Aaaaachhhhk . . ." said the woman. It was a sort of grunt and gurgle at the same time.

Holy crap! I have a heckler.

I've had people react to my talks before, but never had they been this vocal.

Don't take it personally.

I looked up at the rest of the crowd and made eye contact with a woman near the back row who was just beaming. I continued to talk and directed almost every word to her warm and welcoming face. The mean lady in the front row continued to make her noises, but I just chose not to focus on them.

That crazy lady's reaction is not about you. You can't take it on.

It was an excellent exercise in discipline to not let that woman's squawking derail my talk; I was determined to keep going.

After the Q-and-A section, I walked toward the smiling woman near the back and introduced myself.

"Hi there," I said. "I wanted to thank you for smiling at me; it really helped me deal with the heckler in the front row," I explained.

"Heckler? I didn't hear anything," she said.

Wow. She was so focused on what I was saying that she hadn't heard the heckler?

"My name is Mary Ellen," she said, holding out her hand. "I have to tell you, I heard you on the radio with *Eric and Kathy*. I never come to these things, but I just had to meet you and tell you what happened," she said.

"Nice to meet you!" I said. "What happened?"

"I was driving my car, and this hawk swooped down and flew right over my windshield, and I heard 'turn on the radio.' I never listen to the radio, but I always think of a hawk as being a sign from my dead dad, so I listened to the voice and turned it on. At that exact moment, you were on the radio being interviewed by Eric and you were talking about your dead dad and your book. I thought 'what a coincidence!' So much of what you said made sense to me, so I wrote down where you were going to be talking, and here I am! Will you sign these?" she asked, holding out a pile of books.

Because I didn't take it personally and fixate on the mean person who didn't like me, I was able to open my eyes to the entire room and appreciate the rest of the audience.

"You made my night," I told Mary Ellen, signing her books.

"Jenniffer?" A woman said from the other direction of the room, trying to get my attention. "I wanted to invite you to our séance next Thursday night."

I looked over and saw a large woman with anxious eyes approaching me.

"Here is my card," she said, handing it to me. "I channel spirits," she whispered.

"Oh, I see," I said.

"But next week, we will be channeling the ghosts of Marilyn Monroe and Thomas Jefferson," she said with a straight face. "We want to get their take on what's happening globally. I really think you would enjoy it."

You've got to be kidding me.

"Thank you very much," I said, trying not to laugh. I looked to my right and made eye contact with my friend Laura. She walked up to me and whispered, "Welcome to the *downside* of the Other Side . . ."

The channeling lady walked away.

"Why me?" I asked Laura.

"Hey, you're talking about reaching your dead dad, hon. Why not bring in some dead famous people for your next book?" she joked. "Marilyn Monroe would be awesome."

I looked around. A few people that I had invited were "no-shows."

One of them I had been trying to get to a talk for months, but she was always canceling at the last minute.

"Where's Deb?" I asked Laura.

"Not sure," she said.

The next day, I was talking to a mutual friend over the phone, and she finally let the cat out of the bag about Deb.

"Deb has issues with your content," she said.

"Issues?"

"Yeah. The whole medium thing. It goes against her Christian beliefs."

Don't take it personally.

I sent Deb an email and tried to explain that if she really was a believer of Jesus, a man who didn't judge and was full of love, then maybe she herself could do the same and just be a supportive friend.

Weeks went by, and I never heard back from her. I tried *not* to pass judgment. After all, this is what I was asking of her, right? However, every time she popped into my mind, I would get pissed off.

One day I went for a run to blow off some steam, but I had a hard time clearing my head.

Who is she to say her way is the only way? Why is she so stubborn and narrow-minded? She is so shallow!

After I ran for a while, still fuming with my angry thoughts, I realized I didn't feel any better than I did before I'd started. My negative energy left me exhausted. Then a conversation I'd had with Deepak Chopra flashed through my mind.

"You see all those protesters for peace, and they are just as angry as the people fighting the wars. Emotions have energy. You have to come from a place of compassion and forgiveness, or you will never be able to find neutrality."

"But how can I feel compassion when I truly feel that someone is being irrational?" I had asked.

"To say 'I'm right and you're wrong' is counterproductive," Deepak warned. "Any judgment, no matter which side of the fence you are on, is still a judgment. You have to make sure that your every thought, your every word, your every action is filled with loving energy. This will have a ripple effect in the mass stream of consciousness. That's how you can make a difference."

"How can I feel love instead of anger?"

"Anger should be acknowledged. It can initiate change. But many people sit in a state of anger, and they choose not to move forward. That's when it does more harm than good."

I tried to think compassionate thoughts about Deb.

Thank you in advance, Universe, for helping me feel grace and forgiveness.

I once had a therapist who told me the best way to feel compassion for someone who pisses you off is to picture them as a terrified five-year-old on the first day of kindergarten. It's hard to imagine yelling at a quivering child. Since everyone has some sort of fear and wound stemming from their childhood, this visual has helped me keep my cool on many occasions. Got a shitty boss? Picture them with no friends for the field trip. Mean ex-boyfriend? Maybe he peed his pants during recess and hasn't gotten over it. We never know the depths of someone else's wounds. That's why you should *never take anything personally.*

"You've done all you can do with the Deb thing," my friend said. "You might not be able to undo decades of conditioning and beliefs."

Thank you for helping me feel compassion and grace when I think of Deb. And for helping me not take it personally.

"I GOT A GIG!" I screamed. I'd just opened an email confirming a video shoot in San Francisco, and I wanted Clay, who was in the basement, to know about the good news.

"Thank GOD!" he yelled back. It had been a slow couple of months, and we'd just gotten our tax bill.

I looked down at my phone and saw that I had a message. When I checked it, I heard my voice-over agent delivering *more* good news.

"Hey, Jen, it's Susan. Can you make it to a voice-over session downtown for Duncan Hines tomorrow?"

Shit!

My video shoot was to take place tomorrow as well.

"When it rains it pours," I said, calling her back. "What do we do?"

"I'm gonna see if I can book this session early enough in the morning so you can do both if you get on a later flight," she said. "This is a national TV spot, so you don't want to miss it!"

"It is?!" I gasped.

The difference between a demo and a national commercial is ... well, *huge*. A national commercial that runs for several months can pay six figures, easy. A demo pays a few hundred bucks.

"I will change the flight, no worries," I said. "Thank you!"

I hung up the phone and went online to see about rebooking my ticket.

"I haven't gotten any voice gigs in months," I said to Clay later. "Now I get two jobs for the same day? Jesus!"

The only flight I could take and still make my shoot in California was at 11:30 a.m. The Duncan Hines session was at 9 a.m.

"They promised you'd be out of there by ten," Susan said.

This is going to be tight.

THE COMMERCIAL was for microwavable brownie mix.

"New Duncan Hines Warm Delights ..."

The copy oooozed of sexy chocolate, which was how I'd delivered it in the audition. So I did the same thing when I got to the recording session.

"Okay, um, can you please make her a little perkier?" the producer's voice said through the speakers. I could see her face scrunch in disapproval through the glass as she heard my first few takes.

"New Duncan Hines Warm Delights . . ." I said, with a hint more smile in my voice. "Just can't wait till that 'ding.'" I gave her several takes in a row.

The producer looked to the man sitting at her left. They had a conference for a few seconds. She leaned forward and pushed her "talk" button.

"Okay, I'm just not feeling her. She's still too sexy. I really don't want her to be sexy," she said.

I guess with words like "ooooey" and "goooooey," I should have known better.

"I'm going to play the music for you so you can try to match the feel," she said. "I really need this mom to be relatable."

"Okay, Jenniffer, here goes the music," the engineer said, pressing some buttons.

I sat and listened to a bouncy tune that could have been an intro to one of my son's favorite cartoons. So *not* sexy.

I looked down at the copy, and reread the description of the voice. "Sexy, sultry."

Somebody in the chain of command wanted "va-va-voom," but it wasn't my job to figure it out.

"Okay. That was very helpful, thanks," I said. "I got it now."

"Here we go," the engineer said. "Take five."

I delivered several takes. They were perky as hell. Hopefully, the producer would be pleased.

I watched her listen to the playback, and she was grinning ear to ear.

"Okay, I think we got it," she said.

I looked at the clock. It was 9:40. If this sucker got approved, I could be on my way to O'Hare within minutes.

Sweet.

"We're just going to patch this through to get approval," she said. I waited as they got her boss on the line. It just figured; he was in San Francisco. He had woken up extra early to approve this because I had a flight to catch, and he was not happy about it.

"Let me hear it," he grumbled, sounding like he was barely conscious.

"New Duncan Hines Warm Delights . . ."

My voice sounded like a cheerleader after too many Red Bulls.

There was a long pause after it was finished, and then I heard, "Who is this woman?! I don't want *this!* This lady sounds like she drives a minivan! These are brownies, okay?! I want to hear yummmmmmmy, sexxxxy, chocolate! *Not* a soccer mom!"

The producer looked both embarrassed and annoyed.

"Gotcha!" she said. "We'll call you back in a few."

She hung up the phone and put her head in her hands in frustration. She leaned forward and pushed her "talk" button.

"Let's go back to the sexy read for now," she sighed.

The guy in San Francisco didn't like my "perky mom," and the producer didn't like my "sexy mom." I couldn't win with either of them.

Don't take it personally, Jen.

"New Duncan Hines Waaaaarmmmm Delights . . ." I said, putting the "sultry" back into the dessert as well as my voice. It sounded so ridiculous with the dorky music playing underneath, but I wasn't going to argue. I had a plane to catch.

"That'll do," the man said when we called him back.

That'll DO?!

I looked at the clock. It was 10:10.

I zipped out of that studio and hailed a cab on Michigan Avenue. "How quickly can you get me to O'Hare?" I asked the cab driver.

I'd basically given my cabbie free rein to drive like a maniac, and I have never been so terrified in my life. I put on my seat belt and prayed.

Thank you in advance for helping me make my flight. . . . Thank you in advance for helping me make it there alive.

I got to O'Hare at 11:05. Thankfully, I wasn't checking any luggage, but I still had to get my boarding pass. As I tried to print it out at the kiosk, a message appeared on the screen saying, "Please go to the gate for a seat assignment." I couldn't get through security unless I had a boarding pass. I went to try and find an agent, but the line was twenty bodies deep. So I did what everyone hates when they are standing in a line—I jumped to the front.

"Excuse me, but my flight leaves in twenty-five minutes, and the kiosk won't give me a boarding pass," I said to an agent, who refused to look up from her computer screen.

"You are cutting in line," a really pissed-off man yelled from behind me.

"My flight takes off in twenty-five minutes, can you give me a break?" I yelled back. He just frowned and looked away.

The agent let out a looooooong sigh as she handed me a piece of paper.

"I gave you a seat, but you have to run. Do you understand? You still have to go through security and then head all the way to the C concourse. No stopping to use the bathroom," she said, almost scolding me.

"Thank you," I said, pulling my boarding pass out of her hands.

Have you ever seen those people running frantically through the airport like the family in the movie *Home Alone*? I always pitied them, assuming they were just disorganized or something.

Silly people, with their coats flopping all over the place as they try not to trip on the moving walkways. . . .

I will never mock them again.

I was now in a full sprint, but instead of running shoes, I had on black high heel boots and a nice dress. (I was heading straight to a video shoot, remember?) I dropped my *US Weekly* and a Kit Kat along the way, but unless it was my driver's license or my boarding pass, I didn't care. I made it to the gate as they were closing the doors.

"There you are," the flight attendant said.

"Yes . . . uh . . . ahh . . . here I am," I panted.

I was the very last person let on to the plane. As I sank into my seat, I was sweating. I was so embarrassed until I got a whiff of the man next to me, who I don't think had showered in this decade.

How can I not take this man's stench personally?

About thirty minutes into the flight, I realized that *he* was really a *she*.

WHEN I arrived in San Francisco, I called Susan to let her know I'd make my shoot.

"That's good to hear," she said. "But I'm afraid I've got some bad news."

"Bad news?"

No. Not today. Please don't give me bad news. We're on a good news kick these days. Didn't you get the memo?

"Did they recast me?"

"No. It's not that."

PHEW!

"But this is a demo after all. I was wrong."

My heart sank.

"All that stress . . . for three hundred bucks?" I said, my voice trailing off.

"Hey, at least it's three hundred bucks," she said, trying to be positive.

Don't take it personally.

"It's so hard to be spiritual when I just saw several thousand dollars blow out the window," I said to my producer when I got to my shoot. "That one commercial would have paid for health insurance for my entire family for at least a year."

"There'll be more," she said.

I sure hoped so.

EMAIL JAN and Kevin right now, Jen.

I was sitting in my car when I got a *hit* that I needed to email some colleagues.

Jan was one of the bosses at the *Chicago Tribune*, and she and I had been discussing a possible radio show that would help integrate some of the writers from the *Chicago Tribune* into WGN radio. I was now a writer for the *Tribune*'s blogging community, and having been a radio host for ten years, I thought there could be some synergy between print and radio. Kevin was the program director for WGN radio. I picked up my BlackBerry and started typing a note to both of them.

"Is everyone free Friday to talk about a radio show?"

Within seconds, I got a note back from Jan.

"I was sitting in a meeting with Kevin when your email came through, and we were literally talking about you. Amazing!"

Jan was a friend, so I didn't think she'd make something like this up. Then, minutes later, an email from Kevin came through.

"Was just talking about you with Jan. Yes, let's discuss."

It's meant to be!

The three of us made plans to meet at a restaurant, and six martinis and six hours later, a radio show idea was born.

"You need women on that station," I said. "We make up half the population, and you don't have one woman host on the number one station in Chicago."

Kevin had just fired the only two female hosts in the entire city, so I had a feeling he wasn't a big estrogen fan to begin with.

"Maybe we could have you *co*host with a man?" Kevin said.

Figures.

A couple of weeks went by, and my emails to Kevin and Jan went unanswered. Then I found out why.

"Hey Jen, did you hear about the radio show they're launching next week on WGN?" my friend asked.

They'd decided to move forward with the show, but they'd hired a totally different *male* host.

"We really tried," Jan wrote in an email. "Kevin insisted on going in another direction."

"I *hate* this business!" I screamed to Clay when I told him the news. "This is like the TV show all over again."

"I think the TV show was worse," he said. "Much worse . . ."

"Jen, it's Marc. Can you make a pitch meeting in New York on Wednesday?" the voicemail said. Marc was a producer friend of mine, and we were going to pitch my reality TV show to an interested network.

I quickly went online and ordered a room from a hotel website. I couldn't believe how cheap it was, considering the location.

"It's right in Midtown," I told Clay with excitement.

There was a lot riding on this meeting. If things went as planned, I was to be the host, the executive producer, *and* the creator, which basically meant I'd get three paychecks.

Finally!

When I arrived at the hotel, I quickly realized why it was so cheap. The heater in my room was not only broken, but part of the metal was bent out *into* the room, so I could actually see Midtown Manhattan. Oh, and it was February *and* snowing.

"We have no other rooms," the guy at the front desk said. "You ordered that room from a different website, not ours. That's not our problem."

"But I will freeze!" I screamed.

"We'll bring you extra blankets," he said, with a "you're so screwed" tone in his voice.

I took the blankets and stuffed them into the heater in hopes of at least taking the wind chill out of my room.

"Why don't you try to find another hotel?" Clay asked when I called home with an update. It was already late, and I wanted to focus on my meeting.

"I need to get some sleep," I said, hanging up.

It was so cold I could almost see my breath. Then I heard some loud banging coming from the heater, followed by a "thud." The blankets I'd stuffed into the hole had fallen to the ground.

What the hell?

I reached for the bedside table and turned on the lamp.

OH MY GOD!

On the ledge of the window was a New York rat the size of most raccoons, staring right at me. Apparently, I was in *his* room. I was so shocked I couldn't even scream. I just froze. It reminded me of that moment in the movie *Ratatouille* where the chef first notices the rat making soup in the Paris restaurant.

What are you doing here?!

I reached for the phone and called the front desk. I don't remember exactly what I said, but I'm pretty sure the words "fuck" and "rat" were in there somewhere. For some reason, I wanted to get my boots on immediately. I don't know why, but I thought high heeled shoes could be used as a weapon in case he came after me.

As I slowly reached for my boots, the rat and I were locked in a staring contest. He hadn't moved an inch since I'd turned on the light. I could see he was breathing quickly by how fast his belly was moving. I slid my black boots on and carefully stood on the bed in a ready position.

I was quite a sight—with my soccer shorts from 1992 (complete with holes and ripped fringe), my Chicago Bulls World Championship T-shirt (also from the early '90s), and black leather boots that went up to my knees. I stood on that bed in my disastrous ensemble for seven whole minutes, waiting for help. It felt like a lifetime. As I tried not to flinch, I wondered why this was happening. If we really are *where we're supposed to be in every moment,* what the hell was the point of standing on a bed, being taunted by a rat? Maybe this was a warning or some foreshadowing of how my meeting was going to go in the morning. Was I not supposed to be in New York? How is this part of my divine plan?

Finally, there was a knock at the door.

"Come in," I said.

As soon as the door opened, I bolted out into the hallway. The bellman entered the room, and that fat ass rat jumped back into the heater where he came from. I stood in the hall doing a little "gross me out" dance, hoping it would shake off any "rat cooties."

"Oh my God, blehhhhhhh ... ewwwwww ... ickkkk!" I screamed.

The bellman packed up my stuff and met me in the hall. It was 1 a.m., and we were heading to another room.

"I thought there were no more rooms," I said.

"I guess they found one," he said.

As we waited for the elevator, I saw him give my outfit the once-over.

"I didn't really have time to coordinate," I snarled.

The elevator arrived, and it was full of drunk tourists. I was hoping they were too inebriated to notice my clothes or the zit medicine all over my face.

We got off at the top floor.

"Ohhh, the penthouse," I joked.

"Yes," he said.

Huh?

We walked down the hall to the only door I could see.

"This was all we had," he said, putting in the key.

"Well, darn my luck," I joked.

It was a huge apartment suite, complete with a kitchen, dining room, living room, and a giant bedroom. I could do cartwheels in this place.

"Let us know if you need anything else," the doorman said, putting my luggage in the bedroom.

You really are where you're supposed to be in every moment.

THE NEXT day's meeting with the reality TV producers went well. My rat story wound up being a huge icebreaker to get things rolling. I treated myself to a Broadway show and stopped at a store to get a bagel and a mini-bottle of champagne to celebrate on the way home. As I poured myself a glass, I thought about how much I wanted to tell my dad everything that had happened.

"God, I hope this gig works out," I said to the empty room. "Please help me get this job, Dad. I could use a break."

I lit the candles I'd found in the dining room and sat on the couch.

I can't believe I'm in this huge penthouse all by myself.

I looked out at the snow falling on Manhattan. Just then, I got this feeling that my dad was close by. It was as if he were in the suite with me.

Are you here, Dad?

"If you are here, Dad, blow out this candle," I said, looking at the candle sitting in front of me.

I kept my eye on the candle, and within seconds the flame went out. *Oh my God!*

I checked to see if I'd left a window open. Nope. The other three candles in the room were still burning brightly.

"If that was *really* you, then blow out another one," I demanded.

I stared at the candles. Nothing moved. I could just see my dad rolling his eyes at my request. "I just blew out a frickin' candle and now you want *two?* Damn, you are *so* high maintenance!"

I sipped my champagne in silence and stared at the remaining candles until I retired to bed.

WHEN I returned from New York, I didn't hear from any of the producers I'd just met with for several weeks. After a few months went by, I turned on the television to find *my* show being aired with a different host and a different name.

What the HELL?

"How is this okay?" I asked Marc when I called to let him know our show had been stolen.

"It happens all the time in this business," he said. "It sucks, but it does happen. Just wasn't our time."

Don't take it personally.

THE HARDEST spiritual lesson for me, by far, is to not take other people's actions as a personal attack. And they come in all shapes and sizes, from a crabby mom at the park to a selfish producer in New York.

"Maybe it just means bigger things are in store for me," I said to Therese one day on the phone.

"If you were producing that television show, you wouldn't have had the same spiritual journey," she said.

"Yeah, but I would have been really rich," I joked.

"Your abundance will come in other ways," she said. "And your richness will come from the inside out."

cardinals, dreams, and goose bumps

Look for Signs

Lady of All Saints Catholic Church responded
to the First Presbyterian Church by posting:

CATHOLIC DOGS
GO TO HEAVEN -
PRESBYTERIAN DOGS
CAN TALK TO
THEIR PASTOR.

"HI HONEY, it's your mom," my mother said through the answering
machine. She started every message saying the same thing, almost
like a song, her voice traveling up and down the scale like the so-
prano she once was. I picked up the phone as she continued, "I want
you to turn on channel 11 right now, okay? It's Wayne Dyer. He's got
a new book out, *Excuses Be Gone*. I think you really need to hear this."

My mom was always tipping me off about any guru or spiritual
advisor speaking on television. I could tell her about an author I
interviewed, but that would be "preaching." But if she saw it on PBS,
it was *sacred*.

"I think he will inspire you, sweetie," she said.

Mom also seemed obsessed with sending me job listings. While she meant well, I was going to scream if I saw one more forwarded email from Craigslist in my inbox.

"This is what you should be doing for your career, honey. How can you get one of these shows?"

She somehow thought that all I needed to do to get a series on PBS was to pick up the phone and ask.

"You're an author too, honey. And you're much funnier than Wayne Dyer," she said.

"It's not that easy, Mom."

I turned on Wayne, and the first thing I heard him say was, "Any excuse that you make is a misalignment."

I grabbed a pen and wrote it down.

Excuse = Misalignment.

"Thanks, Mom," I said, hurrying to get off the phone. "I can't watch this right now. I've got to go."

"Oh really? What are you up to?" she asked, probably hoping my answer would be, "I'm interviewing with CBS to get my old job back." While Mom always supported my choices, she still had a hard time understanding why I walked out on a nice-paying network gig with benefits. (Most people wondered, actually.)

"I have another talk in Woodstock," I said.

The bookstore in downtown Woodstock had organized a "dinner, talk, and book signing with Jen" event at the local Italian restaurant. Seventy women were coming to share lasagna and spiritual conversation.

"Okay. Have fun, sweetie," Mom said before hanging up.

As I was making the hour-and-a-half drive to Woodstock, my cell phone rang. I looked down at the caller ID, and it was my mom again.

"Yeah, Mom?" I said.

"You know, honey, I have been thinking about this. Forget the PBS special. You really need to get back onto the stage," she said.

First my old friend James brought this up, and now my mom. Coincidentally, I had just met with an actor friend of mine named Stef to discuss the possibility of doing my one-woman show with a new theater company in Chicago.

"I haven't done a show in over ten years, Mom," I said.

"So. You do talks in auditoriums all the time. That's being on stage."

"I just don't know if I have the time right now."

"Hey, remember Wayne Dyer?" My mom was now throwing the bestselling author's words in my face. "Any excuse is a misalignment."

Am I really making excuses? I have been really busy.

"If you really want to do this, honey, you will find the time to do it," she said.

"Thanks, Mom."

"And I just sent you a link for a 'host position' job with QVC."

"QVC? Mom, I don't want to sell jewelry with Joan Rivers," I sighed.

"Okay, okay. I was just trying to help," she said, getting defensive.

"I know. I appreciate it. I'll talk to you soon."

I hung up the phone and started overanalyzing.

Where would I even begin? Would Stef really be the guy to help me? Could I pull off a show? What if it wasn't good?

I was sort of spacing out as I drove, looking out at the cornfields, while my inner monologue continued.

Can you give me a sign if I'm supposed to do this show?

Woodstock is smack in the middle of farm country, and I was approaching my destination. I noticed a billboard of a man sitting in the seat of a plane promoting an airline up ahead.

STEF?!

I couldn't believe what I was seeing. A giant-sized version of my friend was staring me down. This is the same friend who had been encouraging me to do my one-woman show. I almost drove off the road. I picked up my cell phone and called him immediately.

"Are you on a billboard? A billboard for an airline?!" I screamed.

"Well, yeah. I haven't seen any yet," he said. "Why?"

"I just saw one. I was just talking to the sky, asking if I should do my play with you guys, and then I saw your damn billboard! There you are on a *plane* taking *off*. Looking right at me!"

I loved the symbolism of "taking off" or "taking flight."

"Then let's get on with the show!" he laughed.

After the talk at the restaurant, a woman I'd never met before came up to me and said, "Jenniffer, have you ever thought about making this a one-woman show?"

When one person says something to me that I've been considering, I think of it as a *whisper in my ear*. When two people bring it up, it's a *tap on the shoulder*. If it comes up a third time, that's an anvil over the head that I need to get my ass in gear.

I guess I'm doing a play.

WRITING THE show wasn't as easy as I thought it would be. I skipped deadline after self-imposed deadline. The clock was ticking, and I had two pages written. Every time I sat down at the computer to write, I hit a wall.

Days became weeks, and I was about to start rehearsals. Problem was, I still had no script.

I need a sign, Dad. Where's my cardinal?

James Van Praagh told me that our dead loved ones often come to us in the form of wildlife, or they can visit us in dreams. My dad always appeared to me as a bright red cardinal. I usually saw one when I needed a little reminder that he wasn't far away.

My dad died on Father's Day in 2001. Every year, the holiday falls on a different date, but always on a Sunday. When Dad died, it was June 17. In 2008, Father's Day also fell on June 17. I was suffering my worst case of writer's block that day, so I decided to take my dog for a walk and see if I could clear my head.

I took walks all the time, but not usually with my dog, Max. My husband and I rescued him from the animal shelter and while he's very loving, he totally sucks as a walking buddy. He tries to attack anything that moves and pulls on his leash until he nearly chokes to death. It's very annoying. But on this particular day, I felt like company, and Max was the only one available.

After being dragged by Max for a while, I came upon a church. It was the same church where my dad had married his second wife, so I was familiar with the layout. I hadn't set foot inside the church since, but for some reason, I really felt that going inside would help me. Maybe getting on my knees and praying would eradicate my writer's block? I also wanted to feel enlightened, and being inside a church seemed like a good place to start.

I tied the dog up and approached the door. I put my hand on the knob and was shocked to find that it was *locked*. I know I haven't gone to church in a long time, but it was a Sunday. Isn't Sunday supposed to be a big day for the religious crowd?

I started banging on the door. When I realized nobody was going to let me in, the tears started to flow.

God, come ON?! What gives? I know I'm not here often, but I just want to come in and pray!

I collapsed onto the steps with one hand pressed up against the huge wooden door. I leaned my forehead on my hand and sighed.

What does this mean when I can't even get inside a church? Even when I try to be close to God, something gets in the way.

I looked through the small glass opening in the door. There were no lights on, no candles lit, no parishioners from the morning services—just empty pews. I reached over to where Max was and untied his leash. As we walked a couple of feet away from the church, Max decided to take a huge dump on the grass.

Not on God's lawn!

I reached down to grab the steaming pile of poop with my plastic bag, tears running down my face. I headed for the garbage cans in the alley behind the church. As I dropped the poop bag in the garbage, I saw a beautiful red cardinal on the fence just a foot away from me.

"CHEEEP! CHEEEP!"

He was so close and so loud that I stopped in my tracks. Since I hadn't seen a cardinal in so long, I thought I'd be relieved. Instead, I got pissed. After I disposed of Max's poop, I walked away.

Just a coincidence.

I thought about the cardinal. After about a block, I heard a voice—and this is going to sound strange, but the voice was crystal clear.

You don't have to go in a church to find me, Jen. I'm right here, whether it's by the garbage can or in the pews. I am always with you.

Instead of relief, I started to feel panic.

Great, now I'm hearing voices? This is crazy!

A moment later, my dog decided to take *another* crap. Luckily, I was armed with a second bag. I walked over to a different alley to throw out the second installment of poop. As I reached a garbage can, I was greeted by another bright red cardinal, just inches from my hand.

"CHEEP! CHEEP!"

I had to catch my breath. Seeing one cardinal was fine, but to see two in a row—the second one less than a foot away from my arm as I was throwing away dog poop—was spooky.

I looked up at the sky and decided to put in my order.

I need your help with writing this show, Dad. I know I have it in me, but I need some guidance. Can you help me get unstuck? You're the best writer I know. Give me some of your expertise, please.

When my dad was alive, he worked too hard, stayed out too late, and got married too often. We didn't spend a ton of time together until I hit my twenties, and that was only because I was able to meet him out at his favorite bars.

When he got sick, however, his priorities shifted. So did our relationship. I remember driving him home from one of his treatments a few months before he succumbed to his brain tumors. Despite his dismal prognosis, he had such a sense of calm. He put his hand on my forearm, and said, "You know, I might not be able to read, or write, or play the piano anymore. I can't even drive. All these things I used to love to do. But none of that matters, honey, because I can still *love*. Love is all you can take with you."

I can't believe he's been gone seven years.

I envisioned my dad chuckling in Heaven over my dog's frequent pit stops. He always did have a thing for bathroom humor. His third wife, Vicki, said that his headstone should be a toilet seat because he spent more time "sitting on the throne" than any other human on the planet. (The only other place that got as much personal attention from my dad was the Billy Goat Tavern.)

When I got home, I headed upstairs to my computer. I sat down and wrote for three days straight. My play was done within the week.

In the days leading up to opening night, *everything* was going wrong. The set design wasn't complete. We were having issues with the lighting. We hadn't done one complete run-through of the show.

Come on, Dad. I need a sign that things are going to be okay! I'm so scared.

I took more walks with Max, and despite his frequent needs to take a shit, there were no cardinal sightings by the garbage cans. I was totally losing hope.

On the night before we opened, I got a call from the theater.

"We have a sold-out weekend!" the owner yelled with excitement.

I hung up the phone and had a full-blown panic attack. Not only had we not done a full run-through of the show, but I hadn't performed on stage in over a decade. If this project failed, I had no one to blame but myself.

Please, Dad. Let me know it's going to be okay.

I wondered how I'd gotten into this mess as I cried myself to sleep that night. Drifting off, I found myself running in a field. There were beautiful wildflowers and tall grasses blowing in the wind. I felt like I was in a Merchant/Ivory film, and Emma Thompson was going to greet me on the other side of the hill. I was headed somewhere. I seemed to know where I was going.

I got to a narrow road that led to the ocean. As I walked on, I could smell the salt air. It felt like the East Coast. In the distance, I saw a small shack. As I approached, I heard music and people laughing. It was a bar; a festive, open-air bar. It looked just like the original Billy Goat Tavern—only this one was outdoors, on the ocean, instead of under the Michigan Avenue Bridge.

I walked up to the bar where there was one empty seat. I looked around. Nobody seemed familiar, but everyone was happy. It was "happy hour," in fact, and remnants of the late afternoon sun illuminated the bar and danced on the water. The bartender looked up at me as if he'd known me forever.

"Hey, Jen! I've got a message for you," he said, as he reached down to pick up an old phone. This phone was a leftover from the '70s, with a thick cord and a rotary dial. He placed it on the counter.

"It's for you," he said with a smile.

I hesitantly picked up the receiver.

"Hello?"

"Hey, Jen! It's Dad!"

It was my father's voice, as clear as day, on the other end of the phone.

"You need to stop worrying, okay? Everything's going to be fine.

You can do this. I know you can do this. Don't sweat it. Everything will come together."

The tone of his voice was exactly as I remembered. Tim Weigel was calling me from the grave. I was in shock.

And of course, he called me at a bar!

"Where have you been, Dad? I've been trying to make contact with you for days," I said through tears.

"Oh, honey. I'm here. Don't think for a second that I'm not here. I'm always here. I can't answer every time you call, but I'll be here every step of the way."

I wiped my cheeks and tightly held the receiver to my ear. It was as if nobody else was in the room.

"I would have reached out to you sooner, but do you know how expensive it is to make a call from here?" he laughed.

I woke up laughing. The dream was so clear, I had to write it down immediately so I wouldn't forget. I could still hear Dad's cackle as I sat up in bed, in awe of my experience.

A couple weeks into the run of the show, I was getting really comfortable with the entire process. One night, I got to the part in the play where I am doing an impression of Therese Rowley as she supposedly delivers a message from my dead dad. As I was about to speak, I felt an incredible sense of warmth come over me, and I got goose bumps over my entire body. I tried to talk, and I couldn't. Then, a line came out of my mouth that I did not write.

"Your dad is sending you an incredible amount of love right now," I said, followed by a "puff" to the side as Therese would do in one of her sessions. "An incredible amount of love."

I took a few deep breaths, and the goose bumps went away. I then got back on track and did the rest of the scene.

At the end of the show, Therese came up to me with a huge grin. She had been to almost all of my performances.

"Did you feel anyone around you tonight?" she asked. Therese was always trying to encourage people to develop their own intuitive gifts.

"Well, I did have a moment when I had to catch my breath," I started to explain.

"That's because your dad was standing right behind you," she said.

"In the section where I come to see you, right?"

"Yes. He was standing directly behind you, and he looked up at me in the audience and said, 'Isn't she great?' He was wearing a bright yellow blazer."

My dad was known for his bright-colored sport jackets. It was a trait he picked up when he was dating his third wife, before he left his second.

"I got goose bumps," I said.

"Spirits will give you goose bumps when they are close by," she said. "You added a line too," she continued, having memorized my show after seeing it so many times.

"Oh yeah," I said, remembering my words.

He's sending you an incredible amount of love right now . . .

As the show was nearing the end of its run, I was sort of sad it was closing. At the same time, I was really ready for a break.

The theater where I performed sat about eighty people, and the first row was actually a group of tables on the stage level. This always gave me a clear view of those audience members. On the Thursday night of the final weekend, I noticed a man sitting in the front row with his arms crossed. He was with three women, and he looked as though he'd been dragged to the theater kicking and screaming.

For some reason, I was obsessed with trying to get this man to laugh or smile or *something*. But the more I fixated on him, the meaner he got. When I reached the part of the show where I describe author James Van Praagh's theory of what happens when we die, this man started to exhale in disgust. He was rolling his eyes and shaking his head. I was horrified.

I tried to *not take it personally*, but for some reason, I just couldn't shake this guy's negativity. At the end of the show, I ran into the dressing room and did not want to come out.

"Uh, Jen, there are people out here waiting to see you," my stage manager said through the door.

Who would want to see me? I was terrible tonight.

I took a deep breath and came out to face the music. To my surprise, that man was standing in front of me with the three women. He was still frowning and had his arms folded, but the women were smiling ear to ear.

"Oh my *gosh*, Jenniffer, that was so wonderful," one of the women said. "We *loved* the show."

I looked at the man, who was staring at the floor.

"Is he with you?" I asked the woman.

She looked over at her companion. He was still looking down.

"Oh don't mind him . . . he just drove!" She laughed.

"We are going to bring a big group back this weekend," one of the other women blurted out. "I can't wait to see this again!"

"Well, he is not allowed to come along," I joked. The man still did not look up. I put my hand on his shoulder. "You sure you're going to be okay?" I asked, trying to make light of the situation. "I promise I don't bite." He smiled nervously, but still refused to make eye contact.

I walked back into the theater, and there was a crowd of people waiting to buy books. Here I'd had a great show, and I almost let my entire performance get soured by Mr. Crabby Pants.

The next day, I met my friend Rob Sullivan for coffee. Rob is an author, life coach, and public speaker, and I was sharing with him my experience about the man with the folded arms.

"I want you to look around this coffee shop and find everything that is blue," Rob said with a smile.

I knew this must be some sort of exercise of wisdom, so I played along. I gave the coffee shop a once-over and found everything I possibly could that was the color blue.

"Got it," I said.

"Now tell me what's green."

Green? I wasn't looking for green! Drat!

I said nothing as I struggled to think of a response.

"When we totally focus on just one thing, we can miss out on everything else around us. Look at how much energy it took to focus on that one man. You didn't get to enjoy the people who *were* there cheering you on. You missed out on positive feedback because you let one person rule your responses."

I looked at Rob and smiled.

"This is kind of a personal question, but are you dating anyone right now?" I asked. I wasn't looking for *me*, but I had a single friend that I thought would be perfect for a positive guy like Rob.

"Why do you ask?"

"I want to introduce you to *Mustard Girl . . .*"

i love mustard girl

Always Talk to Dead People

Lady of All Saints Catholic Church
responded to the First Presbyterian
Church by posting the following:

"You have to meet my friend Jennifer Connor," my friend Joyce said. "You will love her. And you have so much in common. We call her 'Mustard Girl.'"

Mustard Girl?

The name alone was enough to get me to show up for the lunch. For some reason, I pictured the CEO of a mustard company to be an old curmudgeon with a mustache and a beer belly. Boy, was I wrong. Mustard Girl had incredible blue eyes, blonde hair, and an engaging smile. She looked to be about my age. When I introduced myself, she gave me a bag containing several bottles of her mustard in every flavor—from sweet honey to Dijon. I picked one up to investigate, and there she was, right on the label.

"You're like the St. Pauli Girl of condiments!" I joked.

If I were gay, Mustard Girl and Angelina Jolie would be my top two picks.

"I just knew you all had to meet," Joyce said, prodding Mustard Girl to share her story. "Tell us how you talked to your dad when everything was going wrong with the mustard company."

When Mustard Girl was an art history major at the University of Wisconsin in Madison, she spent a lot of time eating at a burger joint where the owner used to make mustard from scratch.

"I would watch him make batches of mustard, stirring them by hand," Mustard Girl explained. "I said, 'You gotta bottle this stuff! It's too good!' I had never tasted anything like it."

Then one day, the owner took Mustard Girl aside and told her he was retiring. He asked if she wanted his recipes.

"I thought, what the hell am I gonna do with mustard recipes?" She laughed. "But I agreed to meet him for coffee, and for several hours, I listened to him tell me everything!"

After many botched attempts at recreating the recipes, Mustard Girl eventually mastered the formula. Her ingredients are all natural (even gluten-free!). Several months and exhausting meetings later, this art history major from Wisconsin was going to be running a mustard company.

"I thought, 'How did I get here? I can't believe this!' But I loved this mustard, and I was willing to do whatever it took to get it into production," she said.

But at the eleventh hour, her partner decided he didn't want to go through with the deal. He was her main financial backer, and she didn't have the funds to move forward without him.

So Mustard Girl hit the road and headed up to her family's cottage in northern Wisconsin to do some soul searching. Her father had died in a plane crash near the cottage when she was just five years old, and she found that going there gave her a sense of clarity. "I always feel like I'm closer to him when I'm up there," she said.

On the way to the cottage, she talked to her dead dad for the entire drive. "I kept asking him for help. My two big signs from him are double rainbows and four-leaf clovers."

"Double rainbows?" I asked. I'd never seen one of those before and thought they only existed in fairy tales.

"They're more common in rainy climates, but very rare in the Midwest," she explained.

When she arrived at the cottage, the grass had been cut, and there were no clovers to be found. As for the rainbows . . .

"It rained the whole time, and the sun never came out even once, so there wasn't a rainbow in sight," she said.

Despite the lack of "signs," Mustard Girl still had this nagging feeling in her gut that maybe she was supposed to continue on the mustard path. As she was getting ready to drive home, she got down on her knees next to her car in the dirt and started to pray.

"I just cried and said 'Please! Dad!! Give me *something*. I need to know if this is the right thing to do!'"

On the drive home, she made an unscheduled stop at a nearby church.

"I saw that they were having a service, so I said, 'Dad, if the priest mentions the word "yellow" in his sermon—if he even says *orange*—I'll take that as a sign that I'm supposed to keep going in the mustard direction. Otherwise, I'm giving it up.' And I took a deep breath, and went in."

She sat in the back and waited patiently. The priest got up to speak. "There are times when we all have doubts about what to do on our journey, and we wonder if we're taking the right steps to move forward."

He had her attention.

"But then, we must remember to have faith in the *mustard seed*, and trust that everything will work out."

She almost fell out of the pew.

"I had to grab the woman in the row in front of me and ask, 'Did he just say *mustard seed*? Am I dreaming?' I couldn't believe my ears. That was *yellow* enough for me!"

Mustard Girl found another business partner, and after a few years of blood, sweat, and tears, "Mustard Girl Mustard" is now in grocery stores across the country.

Mustard Girl and I have been friends since that first lunch. Not only can she drink me under the table, but I truly believe there's crack in her mustard because I put it on *everything* ... eggs, chips, carrots, pretzels, you name it. I can't get enough of the stuff. (Particularly the Dijon flavor.)

A FEW weeks after meeting Mustard Girl, I was invited to go on a vacation with some family friends. We were flying in one of those private planes that seats ten people. Since I'm afraid to fly, sedation is usually required to get me on board.

As we arrived at the airport, a storm hit. Not just any storm, but the kind of storm in which the wind is so strong, the trees bend parallel to the ground. My nervousness increased when I saw our pilot approach us in the waiting area. He *might* have been twenty-two years old, and he looked like a cast member from *The Hills*.

"We can't take off until this blows over," he said. I glanced around the lobby for my security blanket.

"Excuse me, but is there a bar in this airport?" I asked.

"There's an espresso machine with hot chocolate flavors," he said with a smile.

Like that was going to help ...

"So there's no wine?" I asked. They had a popcorn maker for the kids for God's sake, so where is the Pinot Grigio?!

He shot me a judgmental look as if to say, "You're on your own, lady." I went into the bathroom at this small corporate airport and tried not to hyperventilate.

Please, Dad. Help me. If I'm not supposed to be on this plane, let me know. I'm freaking out here, and I need to know you are with me.

After my little talk with myself, I realized that getting a sign from Dad was pretty unrealistic. Cardinals and double rainbows aren't things you find inside a small corporate airport. Even outside, the storm was so intense that the birds were hiding out for safety. My heart was racing as I tried to find a way to get out of this flight.

Maybe we can rent a car and drive to Rhode Island?

I heard loud claps of thunder as I walked back to the waiting area. I tried to get my mind off the storm by watching Larry King. He was interviewing medium and psychic Sylvia Browne. Coincidentally, the subject of the show was "Can You Talk to Dead People?"

My friend's teenage son George looked up at the monitor as he chose his hot chocolate flavor from the fancy machine.

"That lady is weird looking," he said, catching a glimpse of Sylvia. "What does 'Irish Crème' taste like?" he asked, before pushing the button.

"It's a hell of a lot better when it's got whiskey in it," I said.

Suddenly, we heard a lot of commotion coming from the entrance of the airport.

"You've gotta see this!" the maintenance guy yelled.

At first I thought there might have been a crash or something, but then I noted that he was smiling.

"I've never seen anything like it," he said.

The girls behind the counter followed him out the front door. I looked over at George, who was glued to Larry King.

"So you kids have been able to see spirits for as long as you can remember?" Larry asked two of his teenage guests. They were promoting a show about kids who see dead people on A&E.

I looked over at the sliding glass door, and there was a group of airport employees just standing in a row, all of them pointing at the sky.

I tapped George on the shoulder.

"Let's go see what they're looking at," I said.

We headed for the door. I glanced down at my watch. It was just after 9:00 p.m. Since it was July, the sun had set about a half hour earlier. As we walked out of the airport, I looked up at the dark sky.

"It's a double rainbow," one of the pilots said.

A double rainbow? In the dark? In the rain?!

"If there's no sun, how can there be a rainbow?" one of the women asked.

No shit!

I stared up in shock at the beautiful colors. They were luminous against the dark grey clouds. It was the biggest, most glorious double rainbow, and it spanned the entire sky.

"I've never seen one at night like this," another pilot said.

There was a hush as we took it all in. We knew we were experiencing something magical.

And I knew then that my plane was going to arrive safely in Newport, Rhode Island.

WHEN I got back from Newport, I was excited to spend the day with Britt.

"Do you mind if I hit the gym?" Clay asked.

"No problem," I said, as Britt and I played with trains on the family room floor.

About three minutes after Clay walked out the door, the phone rang. I looked down at the caller ID and didn't recognize the number. It was an out-of-state call, so I answered.

"Hello?"

"Hi, Jenniffer, your interview is coming up in about two minutes. We're just finishing up a commercial break, and then you'll be introduced," the voice said.

I froze. Apparently I had forgotten to add this interview to my schedule, and now I was forced to not only have a conversation, but a very compelling one, while trying to make sure my son didn't scream "Elmo is red!" in the background.

I felt my pulse start to race.

Maybe Clay isn't at the gym yet, and I can text him to come home?

I sprinted across the room to find my BlackBerry and speedily sent him a text. I was thirty seconds away from being on the air and had an overactive toddler on my hands.

I am so screwed!

I stared down at my BlackBerry. Nothing.

Damn it!

"Welcome back," the voice on the phone said. "I am so honored to have our next guest join us for today's interview . . ."

I looked over at Britt, who was jumping around to an episode of *Fireman Sam.*

Please come back, Clay. Please look down at your cell phone.

I tried to *visualize* my husband suddenly getting the urge to check his phone. My hope was that if I concentrated hard enough, I could *make* it happen.

Look at your phone, Clay. Look at your phone.

"So tell me, Jenniffer, what made you decide to quit your broadcasting job and go on a quest to reach your father on the Other Side?" the interviewer said.

I started talking while running upstairs at the same time to arm myself with various "Britt emergency supplies." Knowing that I had a limited window before he got bored with his show, I grabbed his *Binkers*, his favorite truck, and some crayons. I have no recollection of what I was saying to my interviewer. I was a woman on a mission.

When I returned to Britt, slightly out of breath, I suddenly remembered a passage from one of my "woo-woo" books.

"We have a whole team of spirits just waiting to assist us, but they can't intervene without our permission."

I have nearly fifteen books on my nightstand at one time, so I didn't know if this was a quote from Marianne Williamson, Doreen Virtue, or Dr. Judith Orloff, but it came to mind clear as day. I had a tough time imagining an angel "posse" just chilling out with nothing to do until I gave them an assignment, but at this point, I was desperate.

"Mommy?" Britt said, pulling on my leg. He wanted to play "hide." I envied my friends who had girls. They could sit for hours at a restaurant entertaining themselves with two crayons and a napkin. Britt needed to run marathons. I looked up at the ceiling and started thinking.

If you can hear me—angels, Dad, Granny, guides, whatever title you'd like—I hereby give you permission to help me in any way possible by entertaining my son. Please play with him. Soothe him. Whatever you've got, guys. I have to do this interview, and I can't do it while playing "hide and seek."

Then I sat down on the couch and took a big breath. I looked over at Britt. He moved from the chair to the floor with his favorite truck.

"Who was the most interesting person you met in your journey?" the interviewer asked.

I started to talk and noticed that my son was now lying on his side, pushing the truck. He was completely quiet.

"So are you glad you switched gears to write books and tell the stories you're passionate about?" she asked.

I paused before answering. Yes, I was happy not working in a newsroom anymore, but I sort of felt like a "follow your dreams" fraud. Clay and I still had no jobs on the horizon, and the tumbling economy rapidly dissolved anything we had in savings.

"Overall, I think it was the best thing for me," I said. "But it still requires trust every single day, which can be tough."

I looked over at Britt. He was still playing happily.

"So are you actually encouraging people to believe in mediums and psychics?"

"I am not telling anyone what to do; I just shared the experiences that happened to me. I didn't make any of it up. I want people to draw their own conclusions."

As I continued with my conversation, Britt played with his truck for twenty-three straight minutes. No chirps about wanting to run or needing to hide. He was acting like . . . well . . . an *angel.*

Whether it was "Special Angel Team Weigel" or just a wonderful coincidence that my son decided to behave perfectly for the exact length of time of my interview, I'll never really know.

But hey, now I know it never hurts to ask!

"Do you think you can make a shoot in Napa Valley?" my production partner Laura asked me one day.

Just in the nick of time.

"Hmmm, let me think—a shoot in wine country? Sign me up!"

I would have to interview people at the Staglin Music Festival for Mental Health Research. Garen and Shari Staglin had raised millions of dollars after their son Brandon was diagnosed with schizophrenia twenty years ago. Now they pull out all the stops for this party, which included award-winning chefs, A-list celebrities, and incredible live music.

"You'll probably get to meet Ron Howard, Glenn Close, and Pat Benatar," Laura told me.

I'm in!

As we wrapped up the first round of interviews at the event, I looked out at the view. I was standing at the top of this picturesque mountain, breathing in the air, wondering what it would be like to see this kind of beauty every day.

Suddenly, my phone rang. It was my husband, and he sounded panicked.

"Binkers is gone!" he yelled. *Binkers* was what my son called his favorite blanket.

"What do you mean it's gone?" I asked. "Where did you see it last?"

"It was right here on our bed, and I've torn the place apart. It is *nowhere*. I feel like I'm losing my mind!"

I could hear the anger and frustration in his voice. I walked away from the crew and tried to find some privacy. "Well, unfortunately, there's not a lot I can do about it from here," I whispered.

"I mean, it doesn't make any sense! I'm losing *everything* lately," Clay yelled.

Over the past few weeks, he had misplaced his cell phone and an envelope full of cash. Losing Binkers would make it a trifecta.

"I think my mom is fucking with me," he said.

Clay's mother Kathy had died five years before. I paused to make sure I'd heard him correctly. "So you think your dead mom is hiding your stuff?" I asked.

"Think about it. They all represent *security*. Money. A phone. Britt's blanket. It would be just like her to try and make a point," he said.

Clay was as practical as it gets. I knew he must have really been fried to even entertain this thought. But "Mrs. C," as I called her, did have a wicked sense of humor. If anyone would try to taunt from the Other Side, it would be Clay's smart-ass mother Kathy Champlin.

"Okay, then what you should do is talk to her," I said. "Sit with Britt in the family room, and say 'Kathy, I love you, but stop messing with my stuff.' And then have Britt ask her nicely, too. Maybe she'll stop."

I couldn't believe what I was suggesting, but at this point, Clay seemed open to anything.

"Jen, the lieutenant governor is ready for the interview," the publicist said, calling me back to work.

"I gotta go. Give this a try and let me know how it goes," I said, hanging up the phone.

We worked for the next hour, and, eventually, I saw that I had a voicemail message from Clay.

"I found Binkers." I could hear a smile in his voice. "Call me."

I furiously dialed him back, Pat Benatar's voice bellowing in the distance as she performed her sound check on stage.

"What happened?" I asked as he answered.

"Well, I took Britt down to the family room and put him on my lap, and I said, 'We love you, Grandma Kathy, but we really can't lose any more of our stuff. So please give Britt's Binkers back.' And then I told Britt to ask Grandma Kathy for his Binkers back, and he did. And then I told Britt to hug me like I was Grandma Kathy. And he gave me a big hug. Then I said 'Now kiss me like I'm Grandma Kathy,' and he gave me a big kiss. And we just sat there for a few minutes. And I got kind of sad. So we went upstairs, and I took one more lap around our room and Britt's room for the blanket, hoping it would magically show up, and it was nowhere. Britt was really whining. I looked at him and I said, 'I'm sorry, honey. I just don't know where it is.' And he pointed to the middle of the floor and said, 'It's right there, Daddy.'"

"Right *where?*" I asked. The suspense was killing me.

"It was in the middle of his room," he said in amazement. "I had just searched his room, and it wasn't there. I turned away for one second, and there it was, out of nowhere."

"Oh my!" I said in awe.

"It was the weirdest thing," Clay said, wanting me to know he wasn't crazy. "Is that Pat Benatar?"

The lyrics to "Hit Me with Your Best Shot" echoed in the background.

"Yeah," I said. "She's doing a sound check. I gotta go, but I'm so glad you found the blanket."

"Me too. Maybe I'll find my cell phone later," he joked.

"It never hurts to ask," I said.

"Oh, and Jenny?"

"Yes?"

"Did you know that *you're a real tough cookie with a long history?*" he sang just before hanging up.

"Is everything okay?" my cameraman Jose asked as I put down the phone.

"Clay's dead mom is hiding shit around our house," I said, packing up our equipment. "I told him to tell her to cut it out."

Jose smiled. He'd read my first book and had a perspective that was more open than most.

"Did it work?" he asked, handing me the microphone bag.

"Apparently," I said.

rock star parking, a tight ass, and your dream job

Just Thank the Universe

First Presbyterian Church responded to Lady
of All Saints Catholic Church by posting:

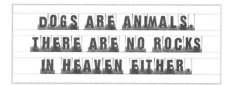

DOGS ARE ANIMALS.
THERE ARE NO ROCKS
IN HEAVEN EITHER.

THANK YOU *in advance, Universe, for the parking space right where
I need it.*

"I can't believe your luck," my friend said, as we pulled into a parking space right in front of our lunch destination.

"It's not luck," I said. "I've changed my vocabulary."

I got this idea of "thanking the Universe in advance" after reading
Conversations with God by Neale Donald Walsch. Walsch writes
that if you say that you *want* or *need* something, you will actually
create more want and need in your life because that is the energy
behind your statement.

"I *want* the perfect job." Or "I *need* more money."

The Universe is just delivering what you're ordering.

The book claims that by assuming that you already have everything you need in every moment, your luck will change. It's just a matter of *allowing* it to find you.

While this all looked good in print, I had a hard time believing that "thanking the Universe" for the perfect job would create that reality, so I decided to start with something smaller—parking spaces.

Thank you in advance for the "rock star" parking space.

Anyone who's ever been to the city of Chicago knows that parking on the street is nearly impossible. Once I started thanking the Universe in advance for "rock star" parking, I kept a small pad of paper in my car so I could document my great parking spots.

Nobody will believe me unless I keep a record of it.

I remember the first day I started my experiment. I had driven to my agent's office. The office is located on a very busy street with a few parking meters, just east of Michigan Avenue.

"Anything's possible," I tried to convince myself. I felt like such a dork.

As I got close, I started to get anxious. "It's only a few blocks away," I thought. "Take whatever you can find."

I saw a car leaving on my right-hand side. I immediately put on my blinker and waited patiently. I picked up my pad of paper and recorded my results. "Holy shit! I found a space a block away. I'm one for one." To me, a block away was a miracle.

When I got out of the car and walked toward the office, I noticed a space open up *right in front* of my agent's office.

I could have gotten even closer if I'd just believed in it a bit more.

After my first success, I decided to drive to every appointment that I had (no matter how close it was to my home), just for the sake of the experiment. Two days later, I was going to my agent's office again. I got in the car, said my "prayer" or whatever you want to call it, and drove off. I tried to just concentrate on "knowing" that I was going to get a space.

"Thank you for the perfect parking space," I kept saying to myself. "Thank you for the perfect parking space."

After making one loop around, there it was: A space right in front of the door. I got out my pad and marked my success. "Two for two. An even better space today." As I looked in my wallet for quarters, I realized I had none.

"Shit!" I said, until I looked out. There were forty-eight minutes left on the meter.

I got a space, and it's paid for. This is fucking great!

After a while, my parking luck became a kind of joke among my friends and family. Going to Rush Street for a night of dancing? Forget the cab, I'll get us a spot. A new restaurant is opening up? Don't bother with the valet; you've got Jen on your side.

My streak was staggering. I stopped counting after 253 perfect parking spaces in a row. No joke!

Since my new vocabulary was working so well for my parking karma, I decided to tackle a bigger issue—my weight.

WHEN I gave birth to my nine-pound, seven-ounce son, I had gained sixty-six pounds in my pregnancy. *Sixty-six!* I've always been pretty active, exercising on a frequent basis, but trying to lose the last ten or fifteen pounds of the baby weight was tough. Normally, I'd consider myself to be an average size for my five-foot seven-inch frame, so this extra poundage really pissed me off.

While I was pregnant, I ate only the best foods and treated my body like a temple for the sake of the child. No booze, no caffeine, no diet soda. I was a "condo" for a kid, okay? It wasn't about me, Jen Weigel. It was about growing a healthy baby boy.

So I started to wonder, why was it okay to go back to eating like crap after the baby was born? I realized that my body is a condo at *all* times. A condo for *me*. Why not treat it just as well as if I were "with child"? Would you put sugar in your gas tank and expect your car to run smoothly? Our body is our vessel. It needs nourishment, not unhealthy stimulants.

I remembered the words of Deepak Chopra about how we can really eat whatever we want if we eat it *consciously*. "The better the food you put in your body, the more healthy items you crave," he said.

Many spiritual cultures have a tradition of blessing their food and have a very spiritual take on meals. One of my friends would place her hands over her plate and pray over her food before eating. I had always thought it was strange and would be embarrassed when she did it while we were out in public. But when I asked her about it, her explanation really seemed to make sense to me.

"If we think of food as nourishment for our vessel, which is this body we temporarily use, it will absorb better into our cells and give us energy," she said.

I'd always considered food an inconvenience that made my ass grow, so this was going to be quite a shift for me.

Thank you in advance for digesting easily and for giving me energy.

Another thing I wanted to improve, in addition to my eating habits, was my body image. Like most women, I've always had issues with my shape. (Boobs too small. Butt too big.)

"You have such a darling figure," my mom would always tell me.

Since the rising popularity of J. Lo, it's now hip to have "back," as they say, but I still wish I had a body like Gwyneth Paltrow (pre-kids). Thankfully, Clay is an ass man.

I thought about the words of *Conversations with God*, and wondered if my use of certain phrases actually had a physical effect on my body. If thoughts really do have energy, was pointing out my butt to myself every time I tried on clothes actually giving it power?

I would eat certain foods and say, "This pizza will go right to my ass." I would tell myself that I couldn't wear a particular outfit because it made my butt look big. I didn't like what I was seeing in the mirror, and part of me wondered if I had created that reality.

I decided that I was going to change all this by complimenting myself on a regular basis.

"Did you know that I have a perfect butt?" I said to Clay. I tried not to laugh.

"What?" he asked.

"I'm going to say it out loud, and then maybe I'll actually start to believe it."

"Okaaaaay."

"I just want to put it out there that my butt is perfect, and I'm thanking the Universe for it."

"Well, I'd like to thank the Universe for it too," he said, giving it a "whack" as he walked by.

As I drove to the gym, I tried to think of a mantra that I could say over and over in my head to help me along.

"I am love, I am light, my body's fit, my butt is tight." I made a little rap out of it. "I am love, I am light, my body's fit, my butt is tight." I made sure that I wasn't saying it out loud, for fear that people would think I'd lost my mind. Every time I got to the "butt is tight" part, I would laugh out loud because it seemed like such a crazy concept. Eventually, I stopped cracking up and started adding verses.

"I am love, I am light, my body's fit, my butt is tight. I'm part of God and full of grace, without one pimple on my face," I'd say, picking up my pace.

After a while, my mantras became second nature. And I swear to . . . well, God, that my body started to change.

"Have you lost weight?" my one friend asked.

"You look great," said another.

When I changed my vocabulary and started eating better, I also noticed that my body started to crave different things.

Deepak was right!

"Do you want a latte?" Clay asked one morning.

"No thanks," I said.

SAY WHAT?!

I had always started my day with a latte. I wondered what the hell was going on with me.

"You are raising your vibration by eating pure foods," my "pray over your food" friend said one day when we were having lunch. "The old way doesn't work anymore because you are building a new container."

Oooh—a vessel upgrade!

Now that she mentioned it, I had noticed that I no longer wanted to drink alcohol as often as I usually did. I went from having a glass of wine a night to having one or two a *week.*

"Don't let this get out to my family, okay? We have a longstanding relationship with booze," I joked.

Another rule that I was now following: *never weigh yourself.* Seriously. The scale is *not* your friend. You could have some soy sauce with your sushi one night, hop on the scale the next morning, and that water you retained will show up in your weight and ruin your entire day! Every woman knows it when she puts on a few pounds. Instead of jumping on the scale, get one "go-to" item of clothing and gauge your weight by how it fits. I have a pair of jeans from college that tell me everything I need to know. Nobody should have their mood altered by a number looking up at them between their toes.

Coincidentally, in the midst of my shifting relationship with food, my husband just happened to enroll in culinary school. He started cooking amazing dishes on a regular basis. And this is hardly low-fat fare. We're talking French and Italian, so lots of cream, butter, bacon, pasta. The portions are always small, and the ingredients fresh. The joy he gets from cooking for his family comes through in the finished product. I am a big believer that just as it's described in the movie *Like Water for Chocolate*, we feel the energy that is transferred into the food from the cook. If the cook is pissed, your meal won't taste as good. When it is prepared with love and attention, it's something you savor. I now eat what many consider to be "fattening" foods on a regular basis, but they don't make me fat.

"The French had it right," I said, eating some of Clay's rabbit ravioli in a red wine sauce. "They eat butter and drink wine, and they're not fat! Thank you in advance, Universe, for this meal digesting perfectly."

When you cherish each bite, you wind up eating much less. And now that I've switched to positive mantras and changed my perspective on eating in general, I eat whatever I want. You heard me. Whatever I fucking *want!* Why? Because when you have embraced the fact that food is indeed *nourishment for your body*, you no longer give power to "forbidden foods" like cookies or potato chips. You also don't overeat. You can have a cupcake, but I guarantee that you either won't be able to finish it, or you won't crave another one. When you are consciously eating, you don't want the whole box of Oreos. You are feeding your soul with positive energy. You don't need to fill your stomach with a pan of brownies.

Dear Jen:
You don't know me . . .

I was checking my emails and there was one from a woman named Clare that caught my attention.

I had to send a note thanking you . . .

I quickly scrolled down the inbox to see if there was anything else I needed to address before getting back to Clare. An email with a subject line that read "JOB—URGENT" jumped out at me. It was from my mom.

> We are looking for enthusiastic storytellers with writing, producing, and interviewing experience.

Sounds pretty good.

> This is a non-paying position, but an incredible opportunity in the third biggest market.

ARGGHH!

Within moments of my reading the email from my mother, she was calling me.

"I was just going to call you," I said. "Why are you sending me job postings that don't pay, Mom?"

My health insurance from doing my one-woman show was about to run out, and like me, she was getting worried.

"If you're going to send me a job listing, Mom, please make sure it's something along the lines of: Cushy gig with great benefits. Not no pay, incredible opportunity."

"I'm just trying to help," Mom said.

"I know. I appreciate it. I'll call you later," I said, hanging up.

I went back to the email from Clare and read the entire thing.

> I was wondering if I could take you to dinner and explain just how reading your book helped me get my dream job.

While I don't usually go to dinner with total strangers, Clare had been given my book from a mutual friend named Amy, so the three of us made plans to get sushi one Thursday night.

"Hi!" Clare said, going in for a hug when we met. She had big warm eyes and an engaging smile.

"So glad we could all do this," Amy said, as we walked in to the restaurant.

We settled at our table and ordered cocktails. Clare then shared with me how my book wound up in her hands.

"Amy kept telling me that she wanted me to read your book. But I'm a really picky reader, so I had it on my bedside table for a long time. Now, you need to know that I have maybe one toe in the *woo-woo* pond, okay?" She laughed. "I am really not into mediums or energy readers at all. Maybe that's why I held off on reading your book, because Amy had told me a little about the subject matter and how she wanted to visit one of the mediums from the book. Then one night, I was walking my dog, and I ran into this woman and her little daughter. The daughter was playing with my dog, and I started talking to them. The woman mentions that she's a CEO consultant. I tell her that I'm thinking of starting a business and could use some consulting assistance. So we exchange information, and I got her card. I emailed Amy when I got home that I'd met this really wonderful lady named Therese who was willing to meet for tea to consult with me—"

"And not just any Therese!" Amy blurted out, interrupting Clare. "Therese *Rowley*."

"Wait, you just happened to meet Therese on the streets of Chicago?" I asked.

"Yes. And I didn't even know who she was in relation to your book because I still hadn't read it yet. I just thought it was a nice coincidence that I needed some consulting and ran into an opportunity on the street. Amy had been talking about wanting to get a session with Therese for months, but I didn't make the connection with the name. Again, I'm not too into that whole thing," Clare said, sort of waving her hand in the air. "And what are the chances that I would run into this woman on the street in a city with nine million people? So I decided to read your book."

After Clare read the book, she started to change her vocabulary.

"It was the part of the book where you talk about how if you say

I want or *I need,* you will literally create more *want* and more *need,"* she explained.

"Because it's delivering what you are asking for," I added. "It's the energy behind the statement."

"Exactly!" Clare said. "But if you thank the Universe in advance as if you already have it—"

"Your luck will change," I interrupted.

"Yes. So every day I would say, 'Thank you, Universe, in advance for the job that brings me one step closer to my girls in Guatemala.'"

Clare volunteered with an orphanage in Guatemala that made jewelry to be sold here in the United States. The proceeds from that jewelry bought food, shelter, and clothing for the girls. This was Clare's passion.

"Things were really going south at my regular job, and I had been told that I might be let go. So I went down to volunteer with the girls on my annual trip to Guatemala and had lunch with one of the organization's founders. He looked at me and said 'How would you like to run our foundation? We are really looking to take it to the next level.'"

Within a few months, Clare left the old job she hated, and now worked full-time for those girls in Guatemala.

"So thank you," Clare said, holding up her drink to make a toast. "You opened my eyes to the possibility that I could really have exactly what I wanted."

As I listened to Clare, I was shocked that my reaction was actually one of total jealousy. Here I was, being thanked for writing about having your dreams fulfilled—as if I had all the answers—and yet I never knew when my next job was going to show up. I had thanked the Universe in advance on a regular basis for parking spaces and my food digesting easily, but was I forgetting to do the same for my career? Maybe I just wasn't doing it enough? Was I not connecting to the intention? I was worn out by all this *spiritual* talk and just wanted someone to call me with a plush contract so I could get my family health insurance.

"You know, I just planted a seed," I said. "You were the one who watered it and made it grow."

I wondered how much watering I needed to do to be in the same boat as Clare.

"I know so many people who have started doing this too, and they are having fantastic results," Amy said.

Great. More people having their dreams fulfilled. Do they need a writer?

"Remember, I wasn't into any of this stuff," Clare said. "But I'm starting to open my mind up a little more now."

"I'm really glad you shared this with me," I said. "I'm going to try to be better about practicing what I preach."

The next morning, as I was thanking the Universe for my breakfast digesting perfectly and *not* going straight to my ass, I added a mantra about my work.

Thank you for the jobs that bring me joy and help me pay my mortgage. Thank you for helping me remember that anything is possible and that there is enough for everyone. Thank you for sending me Clare and Amy so I could be reminded this. Thank you.

don't drink the kool-aid

How to NOT Get Lost in a Guru . . .

Lady of All Saints Catholic Church posts their
final response to the First Presbyterian Church:

**ALL ROCKS
GO TO HEAVEN.**

"I'M PREGNANT!" my friend Julie yelled into the phone.

She had tried everything—in vitro to fertility clinics—to conceive. Nothing worked. As a last resort, she decided to get a reading with Therese. Since she was raised a Christian, she only went when she heard that Therese was Catholic.

"How bad could it be?" she'd joked.

Therese had looked at Julie's energy and saw that she was the emotional caretaker for *both* of her parents, and because of this exhausting role, part of her subconscious did not want to become a mom to a new baby.

"You're already taking on so much. Subconsciously caregiving is your whole identity, but there is more to you than this role. Also, there is a wound in you about having a child that you have not yet released—for which you have not forgiven yourself," Therese told her.

The other big revelation was that Julie had gotten an abortion in her teens, and so she thought she didn't deserve to be a mom.

"God loves you and wants you to be a mother. When you can forgive yourself, the child will come through," Therese told her.

Two months later, Julie was pregnant.

"I am so happy for you," I said, as Julie shared her reading with me. "Isn't it wild how much our own judgments and guilt get in the way of our finding happiness?"

"I wasn't a believer before, but I am now," she said.

After hanging up with Julie, I decided that it was time to get myself an energetic "tune-up."

"Hey, Therese, it's Jen," I said, leaving a voicemail. "I need a reading."

I had been getting a couple readings a year with Therese since I'd met her in 2001. If I was having issues with my family or an argument with a colleague, a quick call to Therese would get them "off my field," and it always made me feel better. I describe a session with her as "spiritual chiropractic work"—only the benefits last for months if not years.

"How about 2:00 p.m.?" she asked when she called me back.

"See you then," I said.

While you don't have to see Therese in person for a session to be effective, I like to see her facial expressions when she's telling me about my past lives, or "soul lessons."

"What are we working on today?" Therese asked, as I sat down in the chair of her office.

"I'm wondering why the work calls aren't coming in," I said.

Therese believes that we all have soul lessons that keep showing up in our lives. Everyone has different soul lessons. If we don't deal with them, they'll just keep showing up in different "window dress-ings." For me, I'd discovered that one of my soul lessons is the *need* to be appreciated.

Therese got centered and closed her eyes. Within a couple of minutes, she started moving her hands rapidly. I kept waiting for a story or for her description of what she saw in my energy field. She said nothing.

"Spirit is telling me not to talk," she said.

"Huh?" I asked.

"You get so caught up in the words," she explained. "I'm just supposed to do this energy work and not talk."

What a gyp!

"But I *like* it when you talk!" I protested. The best part about a reading with Therese was the audio file you could take home and share with others.

"You are becoming too dependent on the words or the stories. You need to be silent for a while," she said. "That's what I'm hearing to tell you."

I started to wonder if maybe she was right. I had gotten to the point where if I was worried about something, I would ask Therese to just "puff" the worry or the person away and then I'd be fixed.

"You forget that you have power inside of you, too," she said. "You're getting too dependent on these sessions."

For the next hour and a half, Therese just moved her hands and worked on my energy. I did feel really centered when I left, but was so sad that I didn't have an mp3 file full of stories to listen to on the treadmill for the next few weeks.

Within days, I got a package delivered in the mail.

"Please enjoy this DVD," a note said.

I had been interviewed on the radio by a woman who was telling me about a healer named Master John Douglas, and she'd sent me his talks on DVD.

"He changed my life," she said.

Master John was from Australia. At a very young age, he could see people's energy and even hear people's thoughts. He says he works with what he calls "Master Angels" to heal, and that he can measure energetic frequencies within the body or spiritual realms.

I popped in his DVD and watched him speak. I've been approached by lots of followers of certain healers or authors since my first book came out, but there was something about Master John's energy and manner that was so soothing. I knew I had to meet him the next time he came through Chicago, whether he "healed" me or not.

"Welcome," said the woman who greeted me at the entrance of Master John's seminar.

She handed me a pile of CDs and some written materials.

"You will really enjoy these meditations," she said.

I grabbed my stash and found a seat.

I've been to my fair share of spiritual seminars, and there was something in the air of this particular gathering that was palpable. Most of those in attendance were die-hard Master John followers, and I was kind of worried they would tell me I needed to throw on a purple sweat suit in order to stick around.

Apparently this was day two of the seminar. I tried to keep my mouth shut so nobody would know I was "cheating" by skipping day one. I listened like a fly on the wall as people told their stories of the previous day.

"I really felt that energy shift when we took the walk in the trees, didn't you?" one man said.

"I have my Location Repair CD running at home at all times," a woman said. "My stereo system broke when I left town for the weekend. And when I came back, the energy in my home was so dark and dismal. I couldn't be in there until I put on the Location Repair."

That sounds like too much work. What have I gotten myself into?

"I had some clients coming in and my iPod was broken," a therapist said. "So I couldn't put on my 'Location Repair.' I told my clients to go home because I wouldn't be able to do my sessions. It just wouldn't be the same."

What's "Location Repair"?

I'm all for respecting someone's talents, but some of these folks seemed to be taking it a little far.

Finally, Master John got up to speak. He had a very sweet face with soft eyes and a calming tone to his voice.

"If you could see how just one negative thought affects your energy field, you would never have one again," he said. "It's like rolling in mud in your Sunday best. Every single one of us has a unique vibration. I can actually see to what degree you are following through with your highest path."

I thought about trying to get an interview with Master John, but what if he told me I was on the *wrong* path?

"In my teenage years, I was able to relieve people's pain by transmitting energy using a hands-on approach," he said. "I didn't really know what I was doing, but I could see that I transmitted love and healing, by intention, through the energy of my hands."

He talked about how he watched a politician run for office in Australia, and he could actually see his chakras close up when he wasn't telling the truth.

"They would constrict and got dark," he explained.

A woman got up to talk of how Master John helped her get rid of Lyme disease. "I am pain-free today, and that's all because of Master John," she said.

He swept his hand over her and could kill the virus, she claimed. The concept seemed totally impossible to me, yet more and more people spoke of his healing touch.

How could this be?

"There is a universal force of energy," Master John explained. "We need to let go of fear and love ourselves. And if individuals haven't forgiven people who have wronged them, they hold on to a lot of locked up anger in their cells, which can cause disease and illness."

A woman raised her hand to ask a question. "I've never asked you this before, John, but I'm very close with my late grandmother. I like to think that sometimes she is watching over me. Do you believe that our loved ones who have passed can help us heal, too?"

Master John shifted his weight and frowned. "Well, there are many dark energies on the Other Side that will want to inhibit your spiritual growth. I would not try to contact *anyone* who has passed away. I think it's best to just leave them be."

I couldn't believe my ears.

Leave them be?

I'd spent all these years telling people to embrace their dead loved ones and ask for signs, and now this healer is saying my research is all wrong?

Maybe I am on the wrong path.

I was about to raise my hand to let them know that I had *proof* that our dead loved ones really *can* help us when we need it. And they don't show up as dark energies. They are *angels*. But just as I was getting ready to unload, I heard a voice say:

"*Not the time or the place, Jen. Don't do this here.*"

I felt like a cartoon whose mouth had been sewn shut. And then I started to feel sad. I thought I knew something to be true, and here was a man who seemed to be quite gifted telling me otherwise. Was I to start believing that all my research was bullshit?

Master John was standing in front of a huge picture window, and as he continued to speak, I noticed a beautiful red cardinal land on the tree behind him.

Nice try. That's just a coincidence.

Within minutes, a second red cardinal landed on the same tree branch.

Just another coincidence. Dad can't give me signs. It was all just wishful thinking.

A third and final cardinal dropped onto that branch. I had never seen three in a row before. I cracked a smile.

Shortly after the seminar, I went to lunch with Master John's assistant. She was hoping I could introduce John to some of my media contacts. While I do have lots of friends working at the networks, I didn't think many of them would be ready to hear about a healer with x-ray vision.

"I have to say, I really don't agree with Master John's theory that talking to dead people is a bad thing," I said.

"Well, he has had experiences with negative energies," she said, defending his position. "The more healing work you do, the more negative spirits show up to try and stop you from doing good work."

"Okay. But if someone feels joy knowing that their dead mother or brother is smiling over them, how can that be a bad thing?" I told her about the three cardinals in the tree during Master John's talk.

"You know, the Universe has a way of touching you in a way that works for you," she said. "If you get assurance from your dad through cardinals, then you will keep seeing cardinals. If someone else needs to see a rainbow, they will see a rainbow. We all have our own unique way of getting there."

She paused to put some more lemon in her tea.

"I had a man call me and yell at me after our last trip to Fairfield, Iowa. He said, 'I don't need Master John's Master Angels to be healed, I can use my own guides and angels to help me out.' And I said, 'You're right. Master John's way isn't the only way to heal. But I think if you *do* use him, it will heal you *faster.*'"

How does she know?

"Master John is a highly skilled healer, and he can do things other healers can't. I've seen it with my own eyes for years," she said.

"I feel like some people get so caught up in a healer, that they can't think for themselves," I said, recalling my own experience with Therese. I tried to choose my words carefully for fear that I might offend. "Can't we *all* tap in to that Universal energy that Master John speaks of and heal ourselves, without needing a guru to do it?"

I remembered one of Therese's favorite Bible quotes, one that she tells me often, from John 14:12: "I tell you the truth, anyone who has faith in me can do the same miracles I have done, and *even greater things than these will you do,* because I go to the Father."

"Think of it as if you were listening to a musician," she said. "Let's say you enjoy John Denver or even Beethoven. You can like their music, but if you try to play it yourself, you won't be at their skill level. They have a gift that they've nurtured and practiced for years. You can appreciate their hard work, but you won't be able to write the same quality of music if you decided you wanted to try being a composer."

"So it's about appreciating and respecting the gifts, rather than getting totally lost in them," I said. "I wish more people used those words instead of *worship.* I think *worshiping* sounds like the ego talking. Gurus and healers should inspire and motivate and teach. But if they insist that you *worship* them, that's not what spirit is about."

One thing Master John did not seem to have was a big ego. But I'd seen many authors and healers over the years preach a "spiritual" game, while ordering around their *worshipful* assistants as if they were gum on the bottom of their shoe.

"I wish I still had my radio show," I said. "I'd interview Master John in a second. It would be very stimulating conversation."

I'd lost my radio gig after I'd returned from maternity leave, and a new boss brought in all his own people.

"I was watching Oprah the other day," she said. "Dr. Oz was talking about how there are physicists who have an equation that proves there are eleven different dimensions happening at once. Then Dr. Oz looked into the camera and said, 'If anyone knows someone who sees more than eleven dimensions, call me!' Well, Master John sees more than eleven dimensions. I don't know how many healers can say that."

Suddenly a lightbulb went off. I was good friends with the executive producer for Dr. Oz on Oprah Radio.

"I think Master John should meet my friend John St. Augustine," I said. "He works with Dr. Oz . . ."

DINNER WITH the *Two Johns* took place a week later. I told "Saint" John about my experience with "Master" John, and how I was both confused and intrigued by his healing claims. "Saint" John had gotten pitched by every healer and author on the planet since taking the job at Oprah Radio, so Master John's résumé didn't intimidate.

As we sat down to eat, I started feeling a burning pain in my left kidney. It had been bothering me for weeks. I'd been to the doctor twice and the emergency room once, and after two MRIs, nobody had a clue what was causing the discomfort.

Unknowingly, I was wincing as we sat at the table, and Master John noticed.

He sort of squinted his eyes and put his hands out in front of him as if he was measuring something.

"Your kidney is extremely acidic. It's at a 10 out of 10," he said, still waving his hands in front of him.

How did he know it was my kidney?

He took his finger and started swirling it in circles, his eyes still squinting.

"Saint" John looked at me and mumbled under his breath, "What is he doing?"

"I don't know," I mumbled back.

At that moment, it felt as if someone was massaging my kidney. I don't know how this could be possible, but I felt something moving inside me, and it was definitely *not* indigestion.

"I'm just putting some healing in here and taking out the acid," he said, still moving his fingers.

"Can you feel anything?" "Saint" John asked.

"Yes. It feels like I'm getting an 'inner-body' massage. It is the strangest thing."

After a few minutes, he stopped swirling his fingers and opened his eyes. "It's still pretty acidic. It's going to take a while to completely move out of your system. You should get some trace minerals right away."

"Trace what?" I asked.

"You can get them at any health food store, and they will help balance that acidity."

"Okay," I said, still processing what had just happened.

Master John continued to fill "Saint" John in on his perspective. "People have many limitations to healing," said Master John. "Their physical body may be filled with dangerous negative emotional energy, which most of us create to varying degrees in our life. The gross energies block up the bioelectric flow in our cells and affect the physical level, causing weakness."

I wondered what sort of negative emotional energies caused my kidney pain.

"To help people break dysfunctional patterns, I work with the Master Angels to replace negative beliefs with love, giving people the opportunity to evolve and heal."

A couple days after our dinner, I went to Whole Foods and got my "trace minerals" or whatever they're called. They consisted of a clear liquid that you put into water, and it was so disgusting that I dry heaved for about five minutes straight after the first swig. But I have to say, my kidney pains were gone within a matter of days.

"I'm starting to think this guy is the real deal," I said to "Saint" John over the phone. "I can't explain it, but my pain is gone, and you know I tried everything."

I could just see Master John meeting Oprah. I wondered how she would react to his finger movements and squinting eyes as he healed her thyroid with the swipe of his hand.

"I'm going to interview him for my show," "Saint" John said. He had a radio show on Oprah Radio every Saturday. "Then I'll give that CD to Dr. Oz and see where it goes."

As I hung up with John, I noticed a woman riding my ass in traffic. I looked down and saw that I was driving the speed limit.

Maybe she has an emergency? I hope everything is okay.

I moved to the right to let her pass. It was a nice night, and we both had our windows down. As she got next to me, she looked over and yelled "Learn to drive!" before speeding ahead.

What a bitch!

I got behind her and was shocked to see that "Miss Impatient" had about five different Jesus-themed bumper stickers. Everything from "Jesus Loves Me" to "Honk if you LOVE Jesus," this woman was a big Christ fan, and she wanted the world to know it.

We got to the light, and I was now next to her. (Don't you love it when the person who blows past you in a hurry winds up next to you at the stoplight?) She was on her cell phone, and totally screaming at the person on the other end.

"That's fucking bullshit, Allan!" she yelled.

I started to feel really sorry for some guy I didn't know named *Allan*. She spewed out more obscenities than one of my cousins after too many Miller Lites. I gave her a good, hard once-over. There was a cross hanging from the rearview mirror. For a woman who claimed to be a fan of Jesus, shouldn't she have been acting a little more, well, *Jesus-y?*

As she continued her rant, I couldn't help myself. I turned down my radio, and I yelled out the window.

"Hey, what would Jesus do?"

Considering this was one of the messages on the back of her car, I figured she was familiar with the phrase.

She put down her phone, looked me right in the eyes, and said, "Jesus would mind his own *goddamned* business!"

The light turned green and her Lexus peeled out of sight.

I have very little tolerance for Christians who treat the world like shit, and then sit in the front row at church every Sunday with a big smile on their face. This woman probably thought that if she repented for being a douche bag, it would undo all the negativity she throws at the world on a frequent basis.

Jesus would mind his own goddamned business?

Maybe so, but do you think Jesus would have ridden my ass or told me to "learn to drive"? Hell no! And while I hadn't been to church in a while, I'm pretty certain he would never, *ever* have taken his dad's name in vain. That's for people like me, dammit!

A COUPLE weeks later, Clay, Britt, and I went to Los Angeles to visit Clay's family. We were staying in a hotel, and just for kicks, I brought my Master John CDs with me.

"I'll do 'Location Repair' in the hotel room and 'Spirit Repair' every morning," I said to Clay.

"Whatever floats your boat," Clay said, tolerating my latest spiritual experiment.

On our first day there, Britt was running down the hall of the hotel at lightning speed and hit his head on the corner of the wall. I could hear the screams two floors away as he made his way back to the room. Clay brought him in, covering his wound, which was starting to swell over his left eye faster than we could find ice and a washcloth.

It was such a helpless feeling watching my son's injury get worse by the second.

After things calmed down, Clay went to see his family, and Britt and I ordered room service and watched *Wall-E*.

As we got settled into our bed with our jammies on, I got out Master John's "Health Repair" meditation CD and popped it into my laptop.

I put pillows all around Britt and myself and made a little "healing nest" as I listened to the words coming from the computer.

"You will be cocreating healing and energetic treatment for your body," Master John said in his soothing voice.

Britt now had a golf ball-sized lump over his left eye. He was lying next to me, sucking on his fingers as he watched his movie.

"Relax and let go," Master John's voice said.

As the CD continued, I pictured angels all around Britt.

Thank you in advance, Master John and the Master Angels, for helping Britt's head get better.

"I request this healing and physical transformation . . ."

It's only an eleven-minute meditation, but about six minutes in, he says, "You will now activate the Master's physical transformation. Be very specific. Some transformation will be instant."

I visualized angels putting their hands on Britt's head and taking away the pain. Just then, the swelling above Britt's eye started going down.

No way!

It felt like I was in the Twilight Zone; one minute there was a bump, and the next minute—no bump. It shrank right before my eyes.

Where did it go?

The next morning, we took a good look at Britt's injury in the daylight.

"Wow, he looks *so* much better," Clay said.

All that was left was a slight bruise above his left eye. No more red line from the impact. No more swelling. It was incredible.

When we returned from Los Angeles, I started using Master John's CDs on a regular basis. From "Location Repair" in the house to "Spirit Repair" in the car, I was becoming a regular Master John junkie.

"This Health Repair CD is really helping me," I said to Clay. "I think you should use it for your foot pain."

"You're not going to try to convert everyone, are you?" he asked.

Clay supported my newfound passion, as long as it didn't mean knocking on doors in the neighborhood.

"Naaahh," I said. "At least not yet . . ."

ONE AFTERNOON, I was heading to a talk at a luncheon, and I turned on the stereo in the car to do my usual "spiritual cleanse" with the "Spirit Repair" CD. The disc wouldn't play.

What the hell?!

I ejected and reloaded it several times. Still nothing.

I got out my CD case and took out the "Health Repair" CD. It wasn't my first choice, but I figured *one* of Master John's discs was better than *none*.

I loaded it into the player and hit "play" and again, nothing came out of the speakers.

"Why won't you work?!" I screamed, hitting my stereo. "This is bullshit!"

I was so distraught, I couldn't even focus on what I was going to say in my talk.

You only have thirty minutes, Jen. Get it together.

As I drove into the parking lot, I took a deep breath and tried to calm down. I realized that I had become so dependent on those Master John CDs that I felt helpless without them.

I remembered listening to that woman at his seminar talk about how she couldn't massage her patients without the Location Repair CD. I was no different from her.

I gave myself a pep talk.

Thank you in advance, Universe, for helping me do a great job at this talk today. Thank you in advance for helping me radiate my truth and speak from the heart. Thank you for protecting me and guiding me. Thank you.

To my relief, the talk was fantastic, and I sold forty-five books.

A FEW days later, my son was having a meltdown in the kitchen.

"What is it, baby?" I asked.

Britt was highly sensitive, and I wondered if maybe he was picking up stress or worry from me, since I was always concerned about work and finances.

I'll just play the Spirit Repair CD.

I ran into the living room, got the CD, and put it on the stereo in the kitchen. As the music played, I tried to rub Britt's back; he wasn't calming down. In fact, his screams were getting louder.

"Boo-boo," he said, holding his stomach.

Britt had acid reflux as a newborn, and he'd recently been having a bit of a relapse. He'd been given Prilosec and Prevacid on and off since he was two months old, and I was convinced that it made things worse, not to mention that it filled his system full of dyes and chemicals. But when Britt had his relapse, the doctor prescribed Prevacid once again.

There must be another way . . .

"Use chamomile tea," Master John told me. "In Europe, new mothers give bottles of chamomile to their newborns automatically. The herbs of that tea naturally decrease the swelling in the esophagus."

I put the teapot on the stove and ran into the other room to find the Health Repair CD. It was nowhere to be found.

Shit. It's at the office.

I went back to Britt, and now he was inconsolable.

"I'm so sorry, honey," I said, trying to hold him. "I wish I could just call Master John so he could wave his hand over you."

His cries got worse, which then made me start to lose my composure. I felt so powerless as I rocked him back and forth. I felt my tears start to drip down my cheek. I wiped them quickly, hoping Britt wouldn't notice.

"Anyone who has faith in me can do the same miracles I have done."

I started to hum, which was a habit I'd used to soothe myself since I was a child. As I hummed and rocked, Britt started to calm down. So did I.

Thank you in advance, Universe, for helping me soothe my child. Thank you, angels, for taking away his pain. Thank you for helping Britt feel safe. Thank you for helping him feel loved. Thank you for helping me feel loved.

Britt stopped crying. Within a couple of minutes, I could feel that we were breathing in sync. The tension in my shoulders disappeared, and we were now slowly moving back and forth like a rocking chair. By centering myself and my energy, I was able to diffuse his reactions as well as my own.

He hugged me tight, and I felt an incredible amount of love pour out of my chest and into his. It was almost as if I'd just submerged myself into a warm bath. The sensation filled every cell of my body. I didn't need anything else in the world in that moment.

I don't think I even knew what love really *was* until I gave birth to my son.

THE NEXT day, I got a message from John St. Augustine. "Call me," was all he said.

I dialed him as soon as I got into my office. "What's up? Did Oprah finally meet Master John?" I joked.

"No, I had a really intense dream, and I knew I had to share it with you," he said.

I remember calling John and saying that exact same thing a few years before when he started working for Oprah. I'd dreamed that I was supposed to tell him: "You are Oprah and Oprah is you. We are all one. Not one is better than the other. Just remember that *your* story is just as important as hers or anyone else's." When I woke from the dream, I got out of bed in the middle of the night and sent him an email before I forgot the message.

While John worked for a spiritual powerhouse, he would much rather be eating a beef sandwich at a Cubs game than sipping green tea on a yoga retreat. Despite his practical side, he did have a sixth sense that was better than most. And he always passed on a *message* when it came through loud and clear.

"What was your dream?" I asked.

"I was with John Denver," he said.

John was friends with the late singer and was devastated when he died.

"We were walking and ended up at a small airport in the sunshine. I had a plane to catch and he said, 'So do I.' Off to the right was a very small one-seat plane that looked more like a little spaceship. He walked over and got in it. For me, there was a huge silver four-prop plane. I got on the plane and although there was no pilot, it proceeded to take off. Then over the loudspeaker came this announcement, 'There has been a crash—we are a landing immediately.' My plane landed . . . and off to the right was John's little plane up against a big stone. I ran over and opened the cockpit; he looked at me like 'what's the matter?' I said to him, 'Are you ok?' He said, 'Yes'. . . and I said, 'Good, because we can't afford to lose you again.' Then he looked directly at me, put his right hand on mine, and said, 'Don't worry about me. You can't afford to lose yourself. Make sure you don't lose yourself.'"

"Don't lose yourself, huh?" I repeated.

"Yeah. I knew I had to share that with you. Not sure what's been going on with you, but I wanted to pass it on. Don't lose yourself, okay?"

"Thanks, John," I said. "As you somehow knew, I needed to hear that."

THE NEXT day, I told Therese about my experience with Britt in the kitchen.

"Sometimes we need to get completely absorbed in something to know what tools we can implement in our daily routine," she said. "We do this in business all the time. You take on a theory or a practice, and embrace it for a while. It's often called The Flavor of the Month. Then you can discern which parts are working best for you, adapt that part, and find more of your authentic self in the process."

I had become so obsessed with another healer's abilities that I forgot I could soothe my own child.

What exactly is my authentic self?

While I enjoyed Master John's CDs, I also applied lessons from don Miguel Ruiz, Jesus, Buddha, and my grandma Virginia. I liked taking a little from column A and a little from column D.

I decided that I'm a combo platter. And I know I'm not alone.

eat, play, laugh

Treat Yourself

St. Cyril Episcopal Church sign:

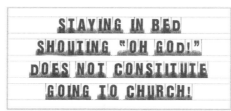

STAYING IN BED
SHOUTING "OH GOD!"
DOES NOT CONSTITUTE
GOING TO CHURCH!

"How DO you stay in such great shape?" I was flipping through the channels and stopped to watch Oprah's interview with Gwyneth Paltrow.

"I work out two hours a day," Gwyneth answered.

Two goddamn hours?!

I almost threw my remote control at the television. I barely had twenty minutes to hit the gym and now this vision of beauty was telling the world, "You too can look like me as long as you have a personal trainer and two hours a day to sculpt your body."

So what does the rest of the world do?

"Why couldn't Oprah do a show about what *real* people can do to better themselves in two *minutes,* and not what celebrities are able to accomplish in two hours?" I yelled into the phone. My friend Missy and I were watching television and talking at the same time.

"So are we taking a trip or what?" she asked. Missy was one of my oldest friends from high school, and she lived on the West Coast. We had been discussing a girls' trip for months, but somehow, life always got in the way.

"Yes. Let's just put something on the calendar," I said.

I remembered the words of bestselling author Caroline Myss when I interviewed her for her book, *Sacred Contracts*.

"Every single person should do a little something for themselves," she told me. "In this society, we think of it as selfish or narcissistic, but really, it's self-*first* and not self-*ish*. It's like putting on your oxygen mask before helping your small child if the airplane goes down. If you do a little something for yourself every once in a while, you will be a better mother, wife, coworker, family member."

"I come to town next Thursday, so let's grab dinner and figure it out," Missy said.

"Oh, I'm introducing Liz Gilbert at the Auditorium Theater that night," I said. "She's the author of *Eat, Pray, Love*."

"Cool!"

"I'll get you a ticket and we can go out afterwards."

IN THE days leading up to the event, I was getting excited. Liz Gilbert had hit the milestones many writers can only dream of. Her book had been on the *New York Times* bestsellers list for two years, and now Julia Roberts was going to star in a movie based on her book.

"Your writing totally reminds me of hers, honey," my mom said. "How come *you* aren't selling tickets for a talk at the Auditorium Theater?"

"It's not that easy, Mom," I sighed.

While my mom was trying to be encouraging, part of me was hoping that maybe—and I know this is really crazy—one of Liz's Chicago friends had read my book and told her that she would enjoy my writing. Stranger things have happened, right?

I was introduced as "Jenniffer Weeegal" by her publicist, so I'm thinking that wasn't the case.

A girl can dream.

"It's actually pronounced WHY-gull," I said as we shook hands.

Liz was extremely easy to talk to. We had the same sense of humor, and I got the feeling that if we had met under different circumstances and maybe had more time to talk, she could become a friend. But this was not the time or the place. I was the gal asked to do a brief intro on her stop through Chicago. End of story.

Now, when I say "brief," let me explain. I was never really told how long my introduction needed to be. I've done dozens of these things before, so I wasn't worried. Liz's publicist told me I could talk about my book and my one-woman show. I would also be able to sell books afterward in the lobby with Liz.

Really? How cool!

A couple of days before the event, I was emailed a script. In the portion that described my role, there was a list of housekeeping things that I needed to say: "Please turn off your cell phones" and "Thanks to Barbara's Bookstore and the Auditorium Theater," etc. . . . I also needed to mention how many weeks *Eat, Pray, Love* was a bestseller (more than a hundred) and how many copies it had sold (six million!).

And then it said: "Jen speaks five minutes MAX."

It was in bold.

I tried to do the math in my head. After all the housekeeping notes, would I even have time to mention my book or the one-woman show? Probably not.

Bummer.

"After Liz talks, you and Liz will go to the two chairs on the side, and you will be given a pile of questions that are from the audience," the publicist told me. "We will have looked through these already, so they will be chosen for you."

They made it so easy.

"Just remember to take the microphone from the podium after you do the introduction," the stagehand said.

Before the event started, Liz and I were standing behind the curtain and had a minute to talk. We were in awe of how gorgeous the Auditorium Theater was, but also how vast the space was behind the curtain. The ceiling seemed to be hundreds of feet away. We almost couldn't see where it came to an end.

"Think of how expensive this is to heat," she joked.

"It's like Vegas," I said. "Beautiful, but so much waste."

I wanted to kidnap her and take her to the bar across the street so we could laugh over some wine, away from the other people, and compare notes. I mean, our journeys are kind of similar in a way. She searched for spirituality in Italy, India, and Indonesia and wrote a book about it. I searched for spirituality in Rockford, Evanston, and Lily Dale and wrote a book about it. Her book sold six million copies. Mine had sold about ten thousand.

See how similar we are?

When I got out on stage to introduce her, I was struck by how glorious the Auditorium Theater was from the perspective of being at the podium. I used to come here every Christmas to watch *The Nutcracker* with my dad. This was an institution. Now I was standing here, talking to hundreds of people.

I started off with the housekeeping issues. I made jokes that cell phones needed to be turned off—after all, I did a one-woman show, and one night when I got to the climax of the play where my dad died of a brain tumor, I was rudely interrupted by the stylings of "Sexy Back" by Justin Timberlake, which had been programmed to be the ring tone on someone's phone.

Don't forget the microphone!

And then I found myself telling a couple of stories. It wasn't really conscious or planned, but they just started to flow. Suddenly, I heard a whistle. This wasn't just any whistle, but a whistle from a stagehand to signal me that I had run long. It sounded like one of those "hey girl" whistles you might hear on a construction site.

Crap! I hope Liz isn't mad.

I wrapped it up and got off the stage. Liz passed me and went to the podium. The publicist smiled at me and said, "You were a little long." I looked at my watch. I had talked for eight minutes.

But that wasn't the worst part. I had forgotten the fucking microphone! I suddenly noticed Liz walking back toward the wing with a microphone in her hand. She had abandoned her eight hundred fans to do my chore for me. I felt like an idiot.

"Is this yours?" she asked with a smile.

When it came time for the Q and A afterward, I sat next to Liz and took out the pile of index cards that had been handed to me. Thankfully, I had watched Liz's talk because many of the questions on the cards were things that Liz had already addressed at length.

So glad I was paying attention.

I put down the cards and decided I would ask my own questions. (I'd already screwed things up enough by forgetting the microphone and talking too long, so what did I have to lose?)

"Now that you've been on this journey for a while, is there anything that maybe you'd wish you'd known ahead of time or wish you'd done differently?"

Liz took a deep breath and thought for a second. "Yeah. It's okay to say *no*. You have to say 'no' every once in a while. People will want you to do things for them or want you to come here, come there. For your own sanity, you have to say 'yes' to you and say 'no' to someone else."

Liz looked out at the audience. "And people will be upset with you, too, or disappointed, and that's okay. You can't please everybody, so you have to practice pleasing yourself. I have this thing I do that I call 'lap therapy.' My cat sits in my lap for twenty minutes every day.

Sometimes this winds up looking an awful lot like a nap," she joked. "But this is my little treat for myself. I have to do it."

Afterward, Liz sold books in the lobby. They gave me a table to sell books, too, but I was tucked under the stairs, far away. I tried to say good-bye, but Liz was surrounded by fans.

Bummer!

"Now about that girls' trip," my friend Missy said as we were packing up my books, getting ready to leave the theater. She was going through a divorce and needed something to look forward to.

"You're right. Like Liz said, we need to say 'yes' to us!" I said.

IN THE weeks before the trip, another friend, Laura, took the bull by the horns, and the "girlfriend getaway" got organized. The location would be Napa Valley. Laura and I had done so much video work for wineries, we were very familiar with the area, so we got a house to rent and booked our tickets.

"I can't go," Missy said, a few weeks before the trip.

What?!

There were complications with her divorce, and having two kids depending on her, she didn't feel she could just break away in good conscience.

I had already taken the time off and booked my flight. I didn't want to turn back now.

"We'll make sure you're on the next one," I said, trying to cheer her up.

The group was originally going to be twelve women strong, but as the event got closer, more cancellations started piling up.

"I can't leave the house for four days," said one. "Work needs me," said another.

The final group consisted of Laura, her friends Nicole and Jesse, and myself. We made appointments for wine tours and had nice dinners. We went running and bike riding. And like most women, we would be laughing one minute and overwhelmed with guilt that there might be something wrong at home the next.

"Why is it so hard to unwind?" I asked one night at dinner.

"Happy moms make happy kids!" Laura said, sipping her wine.

We headed over to a winery for a tasting, and as things got underway, a group of three women joined the tour after it had started.

"Shhhhhh," one of them said to her friend in that annoying *drunk person* way, complete with the finger on the lips. They were trying to be respectful to the tour that was already in progress, but it was too late.

I glanced over at our new tour companions. They were all attractive, complete with low-cut dresses, lots of makeup, and *huge* cans.

BRRRRRRRRINNNNNG.

The chirp of a cell phone got all of our attention.

"Hay-low?" one of the drunk women said in a thick southern drawl as she answered the call.

"I'm going to hit them over the head with a wine bottle," I whispered to Nicole.

"I've got your back," she joked.

As one of the offending women chatted on her phone, the other two had such an attack of the giggles that they literally *snorted*. None of them could walk without wobbling.

"You have got to be kidding me!" I whispered to Laura.

Our tour guide was so entranced with their cleavage, he probably thought they were *charming*.

When the tour was over, we were all chatting in the tasting room, and Laura started to make friends. "So how did you hear about this vineyard?" she asked the "Texas Trio."

"Please forgive us," said the one brunette in the group. "We've been tasting since 9 a.m."

Well knock me over with a feather!

"It's my mom's fiftieth birthday," said the younger blonde next to her.

I did a double take on the mom—a stunning, brown-haired woman who looked about thirty-five.

"What's your secret?" I asked.

"Wine," she laughed. "And trips with the girls."

After talking to them for a good while, we found out that they were actually lovely people—just totally overserved. In fact, we liked them so much, we invited them to join us later for dinner. I felt like a total asshole for wanting to physically *harm* them earlier in the day.

"Never judge a book by its cover," Laura said as we drove away.

When we got to dinner and ordered some appetizers to pass around, our new friends quickly joined us. Within minutes, we were telling one another our life stories.

Jesse and Nicole were both going through separations. Kids were involved, and it was complicated. Laura was divorced with three kids. I was the only married woman at the table.

Then the brunette birthday girl spoke up. "I have just gone through a divorce," she said.

I looked over at her daughter.

"How did you take it?" I asked her.

"I wanted them to get divorced for years!" she said. "I knew my parents would be better as friends."

"My daughter knows me so well," the mother said. "I had filed for divorce without even telling the kids, and that same day, she forwarded me an email called 'The Seven Stages of Divorce' and wrote, 'Which stage are you in, Mom?' I couldn't believe that she knew before I even told her."

"So you weren't upset that they split?" I asked the daughter. "I just think it's great to hear the kids' perspective, since we have two peo-ple at this table going through this now, and they both have kids."

"Kids know," she said. "We know what's really going on. We know if you're really happy. I wanted my mother to be happy. I have so much more respect for her since she chose to love herself and be happy." Her eyes started to well up as she spoke. "You have to follow your heart and love yourself before you can truly love anyone else."

Her mother leaned over and kissed her daughter's cheek.

I got out an old receipt from my purse and wrote down her words so I wouldn't forget them.

god damn! i'm priest certified!

Let It Go

Goodwood United Church sign:

FREE COFFEE.
EVERLASTING LIFE.
YES, MEMBERSHIP
HAS ITS PRIVILEGES.

THANK YOU *in advance, Universe, for the job that pays my mortgage, where I can have fun, and be myself.*

My one-woman show had been closed for months, so my orders to the Universe were increasing daily.

"If you could do anything you want, what would it be?" Therese asked over the phone. "I want to start praying for your abundance."

Therese was a Catholic who attended Mass almost every day, so prayer was a big part of her routine. For me, I had to be *reminded.*

"I wish I had your discipline," I said. "I spent weekends with my dad when I was a kid, and only attended church when he decided to get remarried."

"Do you ever pray for him?" Therese asked.

"What?"

"Your dad. Do you ever pray for your dad?"

I was confused. I didn't think dead people needed my prayers.

"Isn't he closer to God where he is?" I asked. "Not sure my prayers will do him much good."

"Even those on the Other Side need our prayers or positive thoughts," she said. "We often ask them for things, but it's also helpful to give in the process. Every time you ask him for something, send him a prayer while you're at it."

"Okay. I'll try to remember that."

"Now, back to your dream job. What would you be happiest doing for a living?"

"I want to be able to get paid to tell the stories that I'm passionate about. From videos to writing, even the play. I wish I could do that show as a full-time job and actually be able to make a living in the process."

While theater was my passion, it was hardly lucrative.

"You remember the movie *Toy Story?*" Therese asked.

"Of course," I said. "It's one of Britt's favorites."

"Well, we are all like the toys in that movie. We are on the shelf, and God knows we are there. But sometimes he prefers Woody and sometimes Buzz. We each have different things to offer, and we won't all get used at once. We have to trust in perfect timing and divine order, remember?"

"Yeah, yeah, yeah," I said, rolling my eyes. My son was swatting away my hand as I was struggling to force-feed him sweet potatoes. Britt was a pretty good eater, but it had to be his idea.

"Noooooooooooo!" Britt screamed as he pushed away the spoon. I attempted to wipe his face to avoid a mess, but he wasn't having it.

"I don't understand," I told Therese. "I am trying to give him nutrition and keep him clean, and he doesn't trust me. It's his way or no way." I looked at Britt and held his dirty cheeks in my hand, "I have your best interest in mind, buddy! Why won't you let me do this for you?"

I heard Therese laughing in the phone. "You are just like that with God," she said.

"What do you mean?"

"He has a plan for you. He has your best interests in mind. And yet you are pushing away the napkin and the sweet potatoes because you think you know what's best for you. You don't like God's plan, so you want to create your own. You are Britt and God is you."

I thought about what she was saying. While I was so worried about income and my "next steps," we *did* still have a roof over our heads.

"You're right," I sighed. "Radio and television were all I did for so long, I feel like when I'm not being utilized for my broadcasting skills, I'm useless."

"You're being used in a different way," Therese said. "God knows you're on the shelf, waiting to get back into the game. He'll come and get you when he's ready for you."

I looked at my son and tried to feed him one more time. He still pushed the spoon away.

"I guess you come by it naturally, sweetie," I laughed.

At that moment, the other line rang. I looked down and saw that it was my broadcast agent, Steve.

"Hey, Therese, I've gotta take this call. I'll call you later," I said, as I clicked over. "Hello?"

"Hey, Jen, I think we should see about putting your one-woman show up in another venue. I'm setting up a meeting with some theaters. Let's get this back on its feet."

Bring the show back? Yay!

Steve was friends with a producer and theater owner in Chicago. One of the theaters was adding a new cabaret space, and the thought was to open *I'm Spiritual, Dammit* in that new venue.

"In this economy, it's the twenty- or twenty-five-dollar seats that we're looking for. I think your show would be perfect here," the owner of the theater explained when we walked through the room.

I looked around. There were workmen everywhere. This place was far from complete.

"When can it be done?" Steve asked.

"Two weeks at the most," the owner said.

Two weeks turned into eight, and the next thing I knew, we were opening the show to a room with bare walls. Two hours before curtain, the workmen started slathering paint around in a flurry. It was total chaos, and I was wishing I'd never reopened the show.

Perfect timing and divine order.

In addition to the paint fiasco, there was no dressing room. Now I didn't need a big setup, just a small spot where I could focus and stay out of the way until I took the stage. The best this theater had to offer was a closet a few steps from the stage. There was no door to this closet, and there were exposed wires inside. It didn't seem like a safe spot to be, but I had no choice.

This is a professional theater?!

We found a piece of cloth to drape where the door should've gone and put a chair inside so I had somewhere to sit. Problem was, since there were exposed wires, I put the chair as close to the curtain as possible to avoid getting jolted. My nose was almost touching the cloth. I felt ridiculous.

Awesome!

The painters threw on one coat with about twenty minutes to spare, and now the whole room smelled like toxic fumes. We were forced to open the windows to air it out, but it was four degrees outside, so we had to blast the heat to avoid freezing our tails off. About ten minutes before the show was supposed to start, I was summoned to my closet so we could open the house.

This is a total disaster.

"I'll give you a two-minute warning," my stage manager Kat said, leaning her head into my closet, her cheek almost touching mine. Thank goodness we'd both brushed our teeth.

"Nice digs," she said with a smirk. I tried to crack a smile, but she could tell I was in no mood to laugh. "Break a leg."

"Go ahead and close the windows," I said. "At this point, it looks like we're all going to have to live with the contact high."

I could do nothing to change the circumstances, so I decided to accept the conditions and go with it.

You're in too deep to back away now. Just let go.

I heard the people start to file in. Little did they know I was just a couple feet away.

"It smells like paint," one woman said.

"Why is it so cold?" another complained.

I took a few deep breaths and tried to get centered.

Thank you in advance, Universe, for helping me do the best show possible for my audience. Thank you in advance for this audience hearing everything they need to hear tonight.

As I sat in my chair, trying to block out the noise of the crowd, I couldn't help but overhear some of the conversations.

"How did you hear about the show?" a woman asked.

"Well, my husband heard Jenniffer get interviewed by Jonathan Brandmeier on the radio, so he went out and bought her book. We both read it, and I went to one of the mediums she interviewed in the book," a second woman explained.

I leaned my head closer to the curtain, trying not to fall off the chair.

"A medium? You went to a medium?" the first woman asked.

"Yes. It changed my life. My daughter committed suicide, and this medium contacted her."

I carefully poked my head from behind the curtain so I could see the woman's face without being noticed. She was a sweet blonde lady with a gorgeous smile and sadness in her eyes.

If I hadn't been on that radio show with Jonathan Brandmeier, and her husband hadn't been listening in his car and gotten my book, and if I hadn't been sitting in a closet eavesdropping . . .

"I just can't wait to meet Jenniffer to tell her how much she's helped me," she said.

Even when you're stuck in a closet, you are where you're supposed to be in every moment.

Despite the "eau de Benjamin Moore" smell of the room, the show went well. Afterward, I went up to the blonde woman and introduced myself.

"My name is Bonnie," she said, handing me a picture of the most beautiful sixteen-year-old girl. "This is my daughter Hilary, and I got to talk to her again thanks to you," she said.

Bonnie and I wound up going to dinner after the show, and she told me her story. Her daughter was a straight-A student, very popular, and didn't seem to be depressed. And yet somehow, she wound up hanging herself. Bonnie and her family were left trying to pick up the pieces of their lives.

"After I read your book, I decided to call Therese Rowley," Bonnie said. "As I was driving in from the suburbs for the appointment, I was talking to Hilary the whole way down. I said, 'Sweetie, I know this is silly, but the only way I will really know if it's you coming through is if you roll your eyes and put your hands on your hips.' My daughter always rolled her eyes and gave me that 'Moh-ohm!' kind of sigh when I told her anything."

As Therese started the reading, Hilary came through loud and clear.

"Therese said, 'This is going to sound sort of disrespectful, but I'm just going to tell you what I am seeing—there is a beautiful teenage girl here, and she has her hands on her hips and she's rolling her eyes saying, 'Moh-ohm!'"

Bonnie's healing began that day, and she now travels the country talking to teens about suicide and encouraging parents to be more aware of their children's activities on the Internet. She opened the dialogue at Hilary's high school and within her community, where they tried to silence the suicide topic for fear of bad press. She has a purpose and feels close to Hilary.

"I still wish I could hold her," Bonnie said, her eyes welling up. "But I know she is right here."

EVENTUALLY, THEY moved my play to a different theater space within the same building. There were no exposed wires, no unpainted walls. What they didn't tell us was there was another event happening in the same theater each night until about thirty minutes before my curtain time. This meant we couldn't run through the sound and light cues before each performance.

On our first night in the new space, we actually had to kick people out of the room.

"Excuse me, but we have a show to set up," I said, trying to be stern, yet still pleasant.

We finally got everyone cleared out, but we quickly realized they had changed a group of our lights. And not just any lights; they moved the special lights that come up when I talk about seeing a butterfly in my bed the morning that my father passes away. My lighting designer had spent a lot of time on that cue with different color gels. We had centered the lights perfectly. And now they were totally screwed up.

"They did *not* mess with my gobo!" my lighting designer yelled.

As she climbed a ladder to try to fix things, I stood in the middle of the stage and just took a deep breath. It seemed that every step we took in this new theater was the wrong one. But if I chose to extend energy on worry, that would just deplete me for the performance.

It's all going to be fine. Let it go. There's nothing you can do about it now.

As I tried to picture myself releasing all control of the situation, I looked down at my feet and saw a shiny object. I bent down to pick it up, and couldn't believe what I was holding.

"What is that?" my stage manager Jen yelled out from the booth.

It was a ceramic butterfly, with blue and orange hues that twinkled as I clutched it in my palm. In my play, I described seeing a butterfly in my bed the morning my dad died. This one looked just like it. I didn't use any props and had never seen this butterfly before.

"Someone left behind a butterfly," I whispered in amazement. "An orange and blue butterfly."

"You're kidding me," Kat said, coming down the ladder. "Let me see."

I held the butterfly in my hand and we just stared at its incredible colors.

"That's your dad saying that everything is going to be okay," Jen yelled. "Seriously. That's amazing . . ."

"Maybe you're right," I said.

The show went off without a hitch, and afterward, we had a reception with some food and wine in the lobby.

I noticed a man standing in the back. He didn't look familiar and was frowning. He was drinking lots of wine and eating cheese.

"Who is that guy?" I asked my friend Stef.

"No clue," he said.

After a while, my curiosity was getting to me, so I approached him. "Hello!" I said. "Did you enjoy the show?"

The man wiped the crumbs from his mouth and said, "My name is Jerry. I'm a Roman Catholic priest."

Oh Jesus Christ!

My heart sank. Not only is the title of my show *I'm Spiritual, Dammit!*, but in addition to my interviews with mediums and my research into parallel universes, I have an entire monologue in my show about how I am trying to find the "perfect" religion. In it, I talk about how everything I've found has some sort of restriction that turns me off. Christianity is too judgmental, and I express concern about the Bible's accuracy since it wasn't written down (or rather chiseled onto templates) until about a hundred years after Jesus died. I know how my family screws up a story after twenty minutes—it's like a bad game of telephone. Imagine what might have happened to the gospels after various language translations with templates getting broken or lost!

"I thought this show was going to be like the play *Late Night Catechism*," Jerry continued with a frown. "This was nothing like that."

I am so going to Hell.

"But I have to say, I was pleasantly surprised," his face was lightening up. "This was *so* much more!"

I sighed with relief. "Thank *God*, Jerry. You freaked me out for a second there," I said.

"I believe that just about everything you said tonight is true," he said.

Exsqueeze me?

"If you really take the time to look at the gospels, you will see it was all about love and *not* judging. And mediums are all over the Bible," he said.

"Can I take your card, Jerry? I have some people that just aren't going to believe I had a Catholic priest tell me that what I'm saying could be true!" I laughed. My friend Deb was the first one who came to mind.

As Jerry walked out, I looked over at my friends, who were still enjoying the wine.

"I'm priest certified, dammit!" I said, refilling my glass.

THE NEXT day, I got an email from my new priest buddy.

Dear Jen,

Thank you so much for your heartfelt performance.

I did some fast research. 1 Sam. 28 acknowledges the existence of mediums in Israel, and while Saul had forbidden the practice, he himself went to a medium to call up the spirit of Samuel, and Samuel is annoyed that he has been called back, but he did come and speak to Saul through the medium. That is just one example. But I also think the Resurrection of Jesus confirms this further stage of existence. When Jesus appears to Mary Magdalene, he tells her not to touch him because he has not yet ascended to the Father. There is plenty in the scriptures to assure you and anyone willing to listen that you are not a kook for exploring this and that you are in touch with something very real.

I wrote back to Jerry, thanking him for the information. And then I asked, "If the scriptures back this up, then why were some religious folks refusing to read my book or see my play because it goes against the 'Word of the Lord'?"

"Those who say this is against the Word of the Lord obviously aren't familiar with all of the scriptures," Jerry wrote. "And they aren't coming from a place of love."

"I wish those who say they follow the laws of Jesus would act more like, well, *Jesus!*" I said in my reply.

"So do I," said Jerry. "Fear and manipulations have ruined some really amazing teachings over the years. If we all stayed true to our paths of trusting and loving God, rather than casting stones on those who believe differently than we do, we would be in a much different place."

"If more priests were like you, Jerry, maybe I'd still be going to church."

"God lives in your heart," he said.

"So whether you're washing dishes or waiting in line at the airport, you don't have to sit in a church to find God?"

"God is love. God is everywhere."

I WAS DRIVING downtown for a voice-over audition the next day, and I pulled right into my usual "rock star" parking space.

"Do you ever *not* get a space?" my agent Susan asked as I took off my coat.

"Never," I said. "Wait, I take that back. Once. I was with my friend Mustard Girl, and we were going to this bar. We couldn't find a space, and she simply said, 'Maybe someone else needed it more?' And when she said that, I was okay with it."

"So once in like six years?" she asked.

"Maybe longer," I said, trying to remember when I first read *Conversations with God*. "So what do we have today?" I asked, looking over my audition copy.

"Bonefish Grill," she said.

It was a funny, lighthearted spot for a national radio campaign. Not nearly as lucrative as national television, but better than a demo.

Thank you in advance, Universe, for helping me book this commercial if it's for my highest good.

After the audition, I went out to get my car and saw someone slowly driving down the street. She was grasping her steering wheel with worry, looking for parking. I waved to her and pointed to my car. She quickly threw on her blinker and clapped with joy.

"Thank you!" she said, as she unrolled her window. "I *never* find parking around here. You just made my day!"

I got in my car to leave, and thought about what she said. I guess I had forgotten that I, too, used to be like that woman, worrying or fretting over whether I'd get "lucky" with the parking gods. But now I never even doubt for a second that I'm taken care of in that department. It's in my bones.

What will it take to get that kind of knowing about your career?

If I just let go of the need to *control*, and to *know*, in the same way I did with the parking spaces, maybe it would shift?

You need to rewire your philosophy about work, Jen!

When I got home, I went for a run and I tried a visualization exercise. I thought of every rejection that I'd faced over the years.

I pictured each program director who'd turned down my radio or television show idea over the years shutting the door on me. Then, I would look to my left and see another door. I opened that door, which led to a glorious path. The path was bright and filled with violet light. When I reached the end of it, I was standing in a large stadium full of people waiting to hear me tell stories.

Thank you in advance for the job that pays me to tell stories that will help change the world.

THAT WEEKEND, I was writing at my computer, and Clay came in to talk to me.

"I'm in the middle of this," I said, barely looking up from my screen.

"I have to ask you something," he said. He needed my attention about one of our video projects.

"Can't it wait?" I asked. "I'm really in the middle of this."

Part of the problem with working from your home office is the inability to put up a "do not disturb" sign.

"No, it can't," he said, getting more upset.

Tempers escalated, and the next thing I knew, we were both in a full scream. Eventually, Clay left in a huff, and I truly wondered if he would return.

I grabbed the dog and went for a walk to clear my head. I rehashed the argument over and over again in my mind. I genuinely felt I was right, and that he was being irrational. The more I focused on it, the more intense my anger became. I arrived at my favorite beach and sat on the rocks to look out at the water.

I can be upset, or I can let this go. Please, Universe, help us forgive each other. Help us come from a place of compassion and love. Help us let go. Help us.

When I got home, Clay was nowhere to be found, and I was a

nervous wreck. I went to my office and tried to write, but I couldn't concentrate. Eventually, I heard his car pull up in the driveway.

Please help us.

Clay came in the front door and walked upstairs to my office. As he opened the door, my eyes were wide and curious. His face looked neutral as he walked over to me and got down on one knee right next to my chair.

"I am so sorry I yelled," he said, grabbing my hand. "I just worry that sometimes you keep searching and reaching outside of yourself for happiness. Either with *this* job or *that* book. Whatever it is." He was serious and sincere. "But all you truly need is right here. Me and Britt. Yet I still feel you don't think that's enough."

I squeezed his hand as my eyes filled up with tears. This concept was totally foreign to me. When I was growing up, the only thing that made you *enough* was your career. Family just brought on pain and disappointment. I had been so caught up in my ego and worry that I had to rewire my brain to even consider the fact that love could provide happiness.

"Thank you," I said, holding his hand. "I'm trying. I'm really trying . . ."

"NOBODY IS calling me back," Therese said when I checked my voicemail messages. She sounded upset. "It's been four months now, and we still don't have this office space!"

Therese was starting the Center for Intuitive Education to help intuitively gifted kids and adults develop their skills. It was now her mission to get this center up and running so she could create camps, workshops, and seminars. I would be helping with all the marketing and video production. But to get started, we wanted an office. The man who was going to donate a space had been putting us off for months, and now she was growing tired of his excuses.

"There are plenty of office spaces in this city," I said, when I called her back.

"I've gone to Mass every day, and I keep praying, and I just don't understand why this isn't coming together!" she said.

"Hey there," I said, trying to calm her down. "What were you *just* telling me? Perfect timing and divine order, missy. God has a plan for you. Don't be like Britt with the sweet potatoes. Just like in *Toy Story*, God knows you're on the shelf."

"I've been on the shelf for years!" she blurted out. "I'm done waiting. These kids need help now. It's time."

I'd never heard Therese this distraught.

"I think *I* need a reading," she said.

It amazed me that someone like Therese, who helped so many people every day, had nobody to turn to for an "energetic tune-up." She might be spiritually gifted, but she was still human.

"Okay, you have to give this to God. Isn't that what you Catholics say?" I joked. "Say, 'I can't see the path here, God, so I'm going to put this one on your desk. You need to show me the path so I stop worrying.'" I didn't really know what I was talking about, but it sounded good.

"I'm going to compose an email tonight and put it all on the table," she said. "Thanks. I'll call you later."

About two hours later, I got an email from Therese. The subject was "Let It Be."

Dear Jen,

I went to the steam room at the gym and on the way out I was composing my email. It was a good letter. I got in the car and turned on the radio that is always tuned to NPR, but I had changed the station a couple of days ago. On came "Let It Be . . . whisper words of wisdom, Let It Be. I wake up to the sound of music, Mother Mary comes to me, speaking words of wisdom, Let It Be . . . there will be an answer, Let It Be."

So I'm not composing any letters tonight. I think I'll just Let It Be.

Warm regards,
Therese

Two weeks later, an even better office space was available for Therese and the center. Sometimes the best course of action is to not take any at all.

pray, dammit!

How to Spread the Light

Donelson First Baptist Church sign:

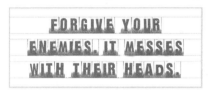

FORGIVE YOUR
ENEMIES. IT MESSES
WITH THEIR HEADS.

"Do we have a decent house tonight?" I asked our stage manager one night in my show's third run with just a few weeks left.

"Not bad," she said. "Not sold out, but a good-sized house."

Just then, my BlackBerry went off. There was an email from Therese saying that she wasn't able to make it to the show.

"Oh shit," I said.

How am I going to bless the space?

Therese had been to almost every performance, which was more than any other friend or family member could say. Before each show, she would come into the dressing room to see how I was doing. Then she would bless the space or say a little prayer for me and for everyone who attended. I had come to rely on her preshow ritual. Without it, I was sure the play would suck.

What can I do?

I didn't know all the names of the saints and angels. But that shouldn't mean I couldn't receive a few blessings here and there.

Or did it?

I was starting to wonder if I was going to be punished. First my super religious friend couldn't make the show, then I couldn't remember the names of the religious icons I should be praying to.

I stink at this.

I peeked my head from behind the curtain to see if I saw any familiar faces. The more people I recognized, the more nervous I was becoming.

Therese once told me a story about a friend of hers who would always say "Come Holy Spirit," whenever she wanted a boost. If she was worried about her job, "Come Holy Spirit." If she was having a fight with her spouse, "Come Holy Spirit." I had a hard time choosing such a *holy* saying to be my *go-to* catchphrase. But remembering the story did give me an idea.

Bring in some light, Jen.

I decided to try and call in as many saints or prophets as I could remember. I'd read enough spiritual books to be able to pull *something* out of my ass, so I gave it a try.

Saint Germaine, Archangel Raphael, Jesus, Buddha, Saint Francis of Assisi, Mary, and Joseph. Oh, and Archangel Michael. If any of you are listening and can help spread the love and light into this theater, it would be most appreciated.

And then I threw some family members in there, too.

Dad, Kathy, Richard, Belva, Ernie, Virginia, John, and any other dead relatives of mine that feel like supporting this performance, thanks so much for your light and inspiration.

Next, I pictured the whole stage and audience being bathed in white light. I visualized my whole body glowing with that light as well.

As I stood behind the curtain, I started to feel completely energized.

And then, something happened. It's difficult to put into words what I experienced on stage that night, except to say that I was completely in the zone. I almost felt like I was having an out-of-body experience. Everything clicked—and in a way it never had before.

As I WENT for a run the next morning, I started thinking about the concept of calling in the light. I had a friend who was a reporter for a newspaper in Chicago, and he did a story on Scientology. While it sounds like the craziest religion on the planet, it always amazed me that highly respected people, such as John Travolta and Tom Cruise, could be members. I also know that the media focuses on just a few facts, rather than telling the entire story, to manipulate our perceptions. All I knew about Scientologists was that they believed in aliens. While that seems pretty wacko to me, there are lots of folks who think I've lost *my* marbles because I talk about having a friend who sees dead people. I didn't want to judge until I had more facts.

There must be some decent attributes in Scientology to attract these highly educated people?

I rigorously quizzed my journalist friend to tell me everything he had learned in his research. His take-away was that yes, they're pretty crazy, but one thing that stuck was that they believe they can heal others by tapping into a *Universal Light.* The Scientologists call it an "assist." If your body is free of chemicals and toxins, you're better equipped to perform these healings on others. John Travolta once talked about getting an "assist healing" on a movie set, and that was what prompted him to look into the religion further. I wondered if tapping into that light could help me when I exercised.

I remembered when Katie Holmes ran the marathon. I wondered how she could go such a distance after training only a few months.

I bet she was using an assist.

While I run several times a week, I can't usually last longer than thirty minutes. Making my way on the usual route one morning, I started to feel sluggish fifteen minutes in, so I started picturing the top of my head opening up and bright lavender and white light just pouring into my entire body. I pictured a bucket dumping violet light over my head, like the water does to that dancer as she's sitting in the chair in the movie *Flashdance*.

Splash!

And then I saw this light travel through my bloodstream with each step.

May every cell be filled with the energy and love of pure light.

I took several deep breaths and then felt a surge of energy. It was as if I had just plugged in to a power outlet. I kept repeating the mantra, and the motivation continued to flow.

"How was your run?" Clay asked when I got home.

"Great."

"You were gone a long time."

I looked down at my iPod. I had run for forty-three minutes.

"Did you put new songs on your iTunes or something?" he asked.

"Sort of," I said.

SINCE I was now bringing in light on a more regular basis, I decided to go through some old files I had accumulated on energy work. I'd taken some Reiki classes a few years back, but stopped doing it when I had my son. Reiki is a type of energy healing that's been around for years in Japan. To do the healing, you must picture certain symbols, and you don't usually touch your subject, but hold your hands just above their bodies. I first learned about Reiki when my dad was sick with brain cancer. He went to a couple of Reiki healers, and I watched in amazement as they held their hands a couple inches from my father's head.

"Do you feel anything?" I remember asking my dad after his first session.

"No, but my vision is crystal clear!" he said, very surprised.

Dad's eyesight had been impaired by the location of his brain tumor, and only after his Reiki sessions did he seem to get clarity.

I pulled out a huge binder labeled "Reiki" from my closet and looked through the pile of papers. I was staring at several symbols that didn't look familiar. While I had taken enough classes to earn the title of "Reiki Master," I remembered being exhausted by all the symbols you had to memorize. Now, a few years after taking my tests, I was proof that "cramming" never lets you retain information long term. You also were not allowed to share these symbols with people who were not studying Reiki, which seemed a little cultish to me. I mean, what if my son walked in while I was studying my folders?

Don't you dare look at my swirls, kid!

My Reiki class was made up of people from all walks of life. From a twenty-five-year-old male personal trainer to a math professor from Northwestern, I loved the diversity of people interested in hands-on healing. When I practiced Reiki, I sometimes saw images—almost like a movie playing in my mind. It was really bizarre at first. I remember working on a girl in class, and I kept seeing a little black dog. She later revealed that her dog had just died.

Maybe it was a coincidence?

One day in class, our teacher brought us a woman to work on who had an illness, but she didn't tell us specifically what was wrong. So the teacher asked each of us to scan her body and see what we could sense.

I walked around the table, putting my hands out like antennae. As I got to her left eye, my fingers started to tingle. I could feel prickling like I'd never felt before. Then I saw a dark brown energy. I thought of my friend James who saw colors and wondered what this meant.

At the end of the class, our teacher told us that this woman had eye cancer and was going to have surgery on her left eye.

Weird.

WHEN I told Master John Douglas that I took Reiki lessons, he said, "You have to be careful not to give energy to the dirty cells, too."

Say what?

"There are dirty and diseased energies in bodies, so to do Reiki on these areas, you can actually give energy to the wrong things. I see this a lot with healers who are not aware of what they are doing."

Oh no!

I believe that if your *intention* is to heal, you won't give energy to the dirty cells, but what do I know? I decided that if I was going to attempt to *bring in white light*, I would not use the word *Reiki* anymore. Some call it *Prana*, and some call it *Chi*. I call it my "*Flashdance* bucket." It's all about whatever works for you.

I WAS DRIVING home from a friend's house one night when I saw what looked like a man lying in the road—and this was on a major street with lots of traffic. A woman was crying over him, and two cars were pulled off to the side. I turned the corner and parked. Apparently this accident had *just* happened, so I called 9-1-1 and walked over to divert traffic.

"Oh my *God!*" The woman wailed, holding what I assumed to be her boyfriend's arm.

He was bleeding on his side and through his jeans and let out an occasional moan.

I asked a few questions and learned that the man who was hit had been running across the street to his girlfriend's car. Meanwhile, another vehicle had turned the corner, and because it was so dark, and the man crossing the street wasn't at a crosswalk, the car hit him. Both the man who'd been hit and his girlfriend seemed drunk.

"I've called the police," I said, crouching down to the injured man's legs.

"I can't believe this happened," she said, still stroking his arm.

I took my hands and placed them on his shoes. I didn't know this guy from Adam, but I wanted to see if I could soothe or ease the stress by bringing in some light.

I watched his stomach as it rose and sank, almost panting. I pictured white light coming from above my head and going into my body and directly out of my hands into his body.

Thank you in advance, Universe, for healing and calming this man with pure white light. May he feel his angels and guides protecting him. May he absorb the divine light in every cell of his body.

As I pictured my *Flashdance* bucket dumping the light, I noticed his breathing start to slow down.

While I know I'm no *Master*, I do think I might have helped lower this man's heart rate.

Within minutes, the ambulance arrived. I slowly got up and walked away from the scene. I have no idea if the man was seriously injured; I just know I was supposed to be there.

DURING MY performances that weekend, I was feeling particularly lethargic.

"I don't know what is wrong with me, but I have no energy!" I told my stage manager.

Before I took the stage, I "called in" the light, as the gurus say, and it did seem to help. But after the show, I was signing copies of my book, and I felt like I was going to fall over with exhaustion.

The last person who wanted me to sign her book was particularly draining. She had lost her husband and wanted me to give her the names of the most reliable mediums so she could talk to him.

"Please, I need his guidance with the kids," she begged.

While I always feel for people in this position, having been there myself when my dad first passed away, I also know that some people get so caught up in mediums and psychics that they forget how to think for themselves.

"There are several different medium interviews in my book," I said. "I think it will bring you some relief."

As she walked away, I almost tipped over.

"You look like someone sucked all the energy out of you," my stage manager said.

I first heard of this "energy sucking" concept from author Dr. Judith Orloff, bestselling author of the book *Positive Energy*. I had interviewed her a few times, back when I had my radio show, and we've stayed friends. She talks about how the "energy vampires" in our lives will prey on us if we allow them. In her latest book, *Emotional Freedom*, she expands on this concept, saying "most of us haven't been educated about draining people or how to emancipate ourselves from their clutches . . ."

She then lists several useful tips on how to protect ourselves from these energetic vacuums. I was doing my best to remember them now.

Okay, take some deep breaths. Stay calm. I think she also said to picture a double-sided mirror on all sides of you . . .

I realized that when I talk to all of these needy people, I have to protect my "energy field," or there will be nothing left for myself.

When I finished the shows the following weekend, a line of people formed to talk with me. It looked like a receiving line at a wedding. I took a deep breath and thought of the words of Judith. I then pictured a double-sided mirror, as Judith suggests, to reflect back any energy that wasn't my own and took several deep breaths before signing my books. Thankfully, I was fine. There was no lethargy and no anger. I felt joy and energized.

Later, as I was taking several dozen roses home from the theater, my stage manager stopped me. "Those flowers are beautiful," he said.

"I'm going to try to make them live longer," I said.

"How?" she asked.

"With light," I said, and smiled.

I got the flowers home and put them into a vase. I'd remembered a bit from the movie *What the Bleep Do We Know!?*, during which they talk about the "Japanese water experiments." The point of these experiments was to see if our thoughts or words could change the look of water molecules as they froze. When water was sent loving thoughts, it looked like a beautiful snowflake under the microscope. Hateful thoughts made it look like a cluttered mess. Since our bodies are 80 percent water, it really made me wonder how my thoughts might be affecting my physical well-being.

Too overwhelming . . .

I decided to start small again, and try it out on the roses.

I grabbed the vase and pictured loving thoughts going into the water. I saw the *Flashdance* bucket dumping beautiful violet light onto my head, into my body, out of my hands, and into the vase.

"Thank you, beautiful flowers, for being in my house," I said, as I took a big whiff of their sweet aroma.

Every single day I would kiss the flowers and "charge them up" with a little light. I even let Britt kiss them, if I remembered. Those flowers flourished for almost three full weeks. I took a picture of them and posted it on my blog to share with my readers. Several people wrote to me and said they, too, talked to their flowers or their plants with great results. Others said it was just a coincidence.

I decided to conduct another experiment. I got two dozen roses from the grocery store. One bunch I showered with light and loving words, and the second dozen got negativity and profanity. I then videotaped my results to post on my YouTube channel.

"Here we go guys," I said, putting each dozen into their respective vases.

I felt really strange holding a dozen roses while chanting, "Shit, fuck, damn you flowers, you pieces of shit!" But it was all part of the experiment.

I placed the two batches right next to each other in the living room. Within a few days, I started to notice the "negative" batch drooping. The positive group still looked good. I got out the camera and took some video of the progress.

"Here they are side by side," I reported. "See any difference?"

Each day I would recharge the positive bunch and ignore the negative. Finally, the negative group started to get crunchy, so I got out the camera.

I brought both vases into the kitchen as Clay was cooking dinner, and asked his opinion.

"I think the results are inconclusive," he said.

"INCONCLUSIVE?!" I yelled. "These are totally dead," I argued, grabbing the negative bunch as they crumbled in my hand.

"Well, the other group doesn't look that much better," he said.

While the positive pile had not fully bloomed, they were still moist and soft. The leaves were green and not brown. I couldn't believe Clay thought the results were "inconclusive."

I WENT FOR a walk the next morning with my friend Kathryn. Kath and I had been great friends in high school, but lost touch for years after graduation. We had recently reconnected and tried to go for a speed-walk every few weeks to catch up.

"I think there is no doubt that your positive flowers looked better," she said, commenting on my YouTube videos. "It's just amazing that some people are in that 'glass half empty' mentality, no matter what the evidence looks like."

Usually Clay was pretty optimistic, but in my flower experiments, he was totally the devil's advocate.

"So I have to tell you, Therese Rowley really gave me some insights about my daughter," Kath continued as we walked.

Kathryn's eight-year-old was having some anxiety issues, which came up in a conversation that Kathryn had had with Therese.

"She told me that my daughter is 'empathic,' which I guess is really common with kids these days. The poor thing is taking on my stress, and even strangers' stress that she meets," she explained.

"So how did Therese help?" I asked.

"She gave me some exercises for her to do before bedtime that will help center her energy and protect her. They're mostly breathing and visualizations, but they really seem to be making a difference."

"She's on a mission to help sensitive kids," I said. "She even has a book proposal out that's a manual for gifted kids and their parents.'"

"I would *totally* buy that," Kath said. "When is it coming out?"

"Well, she hasn't gotten a publisher yet."

"You have to tell me when it's out."

"I will," I promised. "You know, when I was a kid, I was just like your daughter."

"Really?"

"I used to get a stomachache so bad when I was around tension, the only way it would go away was if I could lie on the couch. I didn't know why it was happening, and now I know I was taking on other people's emotions."

"All you needed to do was call in some light," Kathryn said.

If only I'd known then what I know now.

a pastor, a nun, and a journalist walk into a bar...

Learn about Your Past Lives

Twelve Oaks Baptist Church sign:

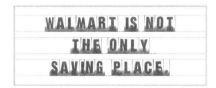

WALMART IS NOT
THE ONLY
SAVING PLACE.

"HI HONEY, it's your Mom," I heard my mother's voice echo throughout the house as she left me a message. "Listen, I think this is a rerun, but I want you to turn on Oprah."

I had boycotted my regular Oprah viewings since the Gwyneth Paltrow incident.

"She's interviewing Dr. Brian Weiss from that book you told me about, *Many Lives, Many Masters.*"

I'd first heard about that book in the mid-1990s from my friend Jacquey. The author got a lot of flack for doing past-life regression therapy through hypnosis. As a doctor and a Yale professor, Weiss put his reputation on the line by publishing *Many Lives, Many Masters.* Now he's a *New York Times* bestselling author being interviewed by Oprah. I'd say he made the right choice by coming out!

The book explains that by learning about your *past* lives, you can figure out why you might have certain phobias or dislikes in *this* lifetime.

I went into the living room and turned on the television. Dr. Oz was talking.

Dr. Oz said that there are certain physicists that believe they have an equation that proves there are several different dimensions happening at once—about eleven. I'd remembered that Master John's assistant had told me about this episode, so I knew it was indeed a rerun. Dr. Oz then mentioned that the universe is separated by shower curtains, and that every once in a while, our consciousness bleeds in and out of these realities, and that could explain these *past lives*.

Are you afraid of airplanes? Well, chances are you died in a plane crash. You feel a weird connection with a person you just met? You probably have known each other for three hundred years. You and your stepmom don't get along? She may have killed you in a past life. The options are endless.

I had learned about many of *my* past lives through readings with Therese. She says they often show patterns of behavior that help us understand certain relationships and why they are playing out the way they are now in *this* lifetime. Maybe you're drawn to a certain era or location? It's likely that you had a wonderful past life in that particular place. If some places make you uneasy, it could be the opposite.

A past life can even explain some physical ailments. I was having severe throat pain and complications from getting my wisdom teeth removed right before the opening of my play. The dry sockets wouldn't heal, and weeks before I was supposed to get on stage, I couldn't talk. Therese did a reading for me and found several back-to-back lifetimes in which I was killed for "speaking my truth." From getting burned at the stake in the Salem witch trials to being hanged during the Spanish Inquisition, my voice was silenced because I spoke out against the mainstream beliefs of the time.

"Oh man, this one is really graphic," Therese reported during the reading. Her face was wincing as if she was watching a horror movie. "They're pulling your tongue out slowly with this torture device."

Great.

"This is an imprint over so many lifetimes that your soul is trying to protect you from making the same mistake," she explained. "It is trying to save you from being punished again."

Whether or not these stories were actually true was irrelevant. By hearing this information, I could release the *imprint* of those past lives and move on.

My mouth was healed within hours.

After watching the Oprah rerun, I decided to pull out some old interviews I'd done with other people who claim to have the ability to read past lives. I went upstairs and started looking through a drawer full of old tapes. As I pulled out a pile, I saw one labeled "Soul Session 11-21-05."

I didn't even remember the session, let alone whom it was with, so I ran into the basement and got out a very old "boom box" to play the tape and refresh my memory.

"It is joyful to be with you today," the voice said. Suddenly, I got a memory flash. Stacy Gorman says she channels a spirit named Jacob, who not only sees your past lives but some things about your future. I personally don't believe someone can accurately predict the future, since we all have free will. Many psychics say that what they are seeing during a session is what would happen if everything continued with the same vibration and intention. But anyone can just decide to get on a plane and fly to Vegas and mess up the whole plan. Caroline Myss told me that "our lives are a combination of choice and destiny," so maybe some things truly are *meant to be.*

This recorded session with Stacy took place when I was five

months pregnant. As with all the "interviews" I conducted for my research, I would only give my first name so they couldn't cheat and look me up ahead of time. Our conversation was over the phone, because Stacy lived in Arizona.

"You have had over five hundred lives on earth—541, to be exact. In each one of them, you learn something different," the voice said.

That's a shitload of lives!

"You never come to climb the ladder, but to have a myriad of experiences. In one lifetime you were a painter. In another, you owned a cheese shop in Italy."

Over the years, I'd been told I was a priest, a Native American, a Mongolian warrior, and several nuns. But this was the first I'd heard of owning a cheese shop in Italy.

I do love cheese.

"From 1586 to 1647, you were a man named Thomas Hooker. He was one of the first people to come to the U.S. to build a new world from Britain. You were a pastor who helped others to understand how to pray or sit in silence with God."

I'd never been given an exact name and date before.

"You preached religious tolerance for all Christian sects. You were an excellent speaker. You are like this now."

How does she know?

"In your current lifetime, you will take a little piece of everything. It is your natural state to go up the mountain with a little belief in all things, that it is *all* God. There is not one particular belief that is correct. That is the purpose of knowing you were Thomas Hooker before."

I hadn't given this woman my full name, so how could she know that I'm "climbing mountains" or that I truly believe that not one particular religious belief is correct? Plus, this reading was done before I'd written any books, done any talks, or performed any plays about this very subject.

"You are also going to change the arenas of children, how children are being educated, how children are being raised; that is going to be your next step out into the world," she said.

At the time of this reading, I was coproducing a video with Therese entitled "The Misdiagnosis of Gifted Kids," encouraging parents to use other means of therapy before automatically reaching for the psychotropic drugs.

"After your own child is born, you are going to go even further, and you are really going to shake things up. But when we say *shake them up*, we do not mean unpeacefully. You will do it in a way where each person will say, 'Yes, we can understand what you're saying, this makes sense, it makes sense for the children to tell us *why* they have come.' Your child that is coming is what is called a *crystal* child."

So maybe that whole talking to grandpa stuff was part of being a "crystal" child?

"You are a writer, and this is part of how you communicate truth," she said. "After your baby is born, you publish a book."

True and true.

"You are going to put out film; films are what you are going to be most known for."

My Hollywood agent dropped me when my dad got sick, and I could no longer fly out to Los Angeles at a moment's notice.

"This will begin after your child is born. There is a man who sets up the foundation. He will become your partner. You will reunite, and he will help with the film."

A foundation? A man? Since I had no male work partner and no hint of Hollywood calling, I chalked that part up to being a "medium misfire."

"Music calms your energy field. You were an artist and you played music, like a lute; you were famous for it," she said. "We believe that Hillary Hahn—she's a violinist in this life, and she was your daughter who died young in that life. We believe it would help you to have her music."

WTF?

I quickly Googled Hillary Hahn and found a beautiful young woman who had several classical albums. I could just imagine making a call to her publicist. "Yes, hello, my name is Jenniffer Weigel, and I'd like to make an appointment to have lunch with Hillary. You see, I was her mother in a past life. I was hoping we could catch up? Hello? Are you there? I'm not a *nut job*, I'm a *journalist!*"

Something tells me that wouldn't go over too well.

"Your guides say that a very big message for you right now is to enjoy every moment and not to look too much into the future. The more you get out of the *need* to control it, the more you get the accurate answer as to where you belong."

Everyone could have this challenge, but again, pretty accurate stuff for someone who didn't know me.

"Keep your eye on the joy," she concluded, "and remember, you can ask us from smallest to largest what you are wanting. We are sending much love with you. . . ."

Her voice trailed off and the phone line went dead in the recording.

I walked into my bedroom, and Clay was just waking up.

"So, I was just listening to some old tapes about my past lives," I said.

"Okay," he said, barely opening his eyes. "So who were you this time?"

Clay had heard plenty of stories about this subject. If I couldn't keep track of them, I surely didn't expect *him* to.

"This preacher named Thomas Hooker. He was one of the first settlers here from Britain," I said. "He founded Hartford, Connecticut."

"Alrighty," he said, slowly rising from the bed. "Anyone else?"

"I was some musician named Hillary Hahn's mother in another life. Now she's a well-known violinist."

"Well, you're a *well-known* author. Call her up for a reunion," he said, heading to the bathroom to brush his teeth.

"Yeah sure," I said, leaving our room.

As I got to the end of the hall, Clay yelled after me. "Hey, Thomas! You want a Starbucks coffee today?"

"No thanks," I said.

I WENT BACK to the tape pile and pulled out one more, this from a woman named Corbie Mitleid. I had interviewed her over the phone about a year after Britt was born.

"I am getting a very strong feeling about something, and this is unusual because this was a well-known woman," Corbie said. "But you were Nellie Bly in a past life."

I knew the name was familiar, but I didn't know how. I hopped on my computer and looked her up on Wikipedia.

"Nellie Bly was a pioneer woman in journalism. She remains notable for two feats: a record-breaking trip around the world in eighty days in emulation of Jules Verne and an exposé in which she faked insanity to study a mental institution from within. In addition to her writing, she was also an industrialist and charity worker."

I read on and learned that they made these women in the mental hospitals sit on cold benches all day long and eat rotten meat. Nellie wrote that many of the women who were locked up were just as sane as she was. She wrote a book about her asylum experiences, and it changed the way doctors treated the sick and mentally challenged.

I stared at the picture of Nellie on my computer screen. We looked so much alike it gave me chills. She was also frustrated by her assignments to cover the "society pages" and "fluff pieces." Her real passion was to tell the stories that mattered and to help people.

She is me!

I went back to the tape to hear more of the session.

"The woman you now work with, who does this kind of mediumship—Theresa? She was one of the doctors in that hospital with Nellie," Corbie said. I assumed she was talking about Therese. "She wanted the other doctors to treat the patients with love and warmth and to walk them around outside and give them fresh air, but instead they beat them and fed them slop and locked them up in straitjackets. I really get the feeling that you two have reunited in *this* life to reshape the way the world sees and treats people with unique challenges."

At the time of this conversation, Therese and I had no plans to reshape the world's view on anything. But now I was helping her with marketing for the Center for Intuitive Education.

I called Therese after listening to my tapes again and told her about how we were The Doctor and Nellie Bly.

"Isn't that wild?" I said. All I heard was silence at the other end of the phone. "Therese? Are you there?"

"Yes," she whispered. I could hear sniffles, and it sounded like she dropped her phone. "Something just happened . . ."

Therese apparently got such a *hit* when I brought up the mental hospital that her whole body bent over in pain. Tears started running down her face.

"I've never had anyone tell me about *this* past life," she said softly. "I really think that one could be true."

Therese later called her mother, a devoted Catholic who doesn't believe in past lives, and told her that she used to be a doctor trying to change the way mental patients were treated.

"Well, honey, that's *still* what you do, isn't it?" Therese's mom said to her daughter. "People come to you and they feel a little crazy, and then you walk them around in the *Light*, and you help them feel better."

I PUT THE tapes away and got my coat.

"Where you headed?" Clay asked.

"I want to see if I can find any Hillary Hahn CDs," I said.

Clay stared at me blankly.

"The violin player."

"Oh yeah, your *daughter*. Gotcha. Good luck with that."

I knew the concept of being Hillary Hahn's "lute-playing mother" sounded crazy, but I was a fan of classical music and my curiosity was piqued.

There were several recordings to choose from, but I settled on some classic Bach and took it home. Hahn's talent was incredible.

I'm so proud!

As I listened in the car, I got goose bumps again.

What's with all these goddamned goose bumps?

I got home and I checked my emails: "Urgent Job Posting."

My mom was at it again.

We are looking for enthusiastic hosts to create real estate videos . . . candidates also need to be able to edit, write, and produce . . .

And shoot and direct and jump out of airplanes . . .

I'd been very disheartened by the job listings available lately, either from my mother or searching on my own. Despite my panic, I had to remember that we still managed to get work *exactly* when we needed it. While it wasn't fun living without a solid schedule or regular paycheck, we did still have food in the fridge.

I scrolled down to the next email.

Please join us for CHICAGO IANDS for an afternoon with Deana Chase-Moore; a massage therapist and past-life intuitive who shares her wonderful and amazing experiences.

IANDS stands for the International Association of Near-Death Studies. Each month at Evanston Hospital's auditorium, they brought in speakers or authors. The Chicago IANDS founder, Diane Willis, had asked me to speak there when my first book came out, and I always enjoyed their events. I continued reading the email.

> Deana has two appointments left on her schedule. If you would like a private session with her, please let me know right away.

I quickly hit "reply."

> Thanks, Diane. I would LOVE an appointment. Let me know what is available.

ON THE day of Deana's talk, I got my seat in the back of the auditorium and listened as Diane passed the microphone around to the audience members.

"Would you like to share with us why you are here?" she asked a heavyset man near the front.

"Hi, my name is Brian, and this is my first time here," he said, with hesitation. "I was in a bad car accident and flatlined on the operating table. I saw *Heaven*, or the *Light*, or whatever you'd like to call it. It was the most beautiful and peaceful thing I'd ever seen. I survived the crash, and afterwards, I had a certain *knowing*, I guess you'd say. My senses were more *in tune*. I knew about things before they even happened. I tried to tell my family about my experience; they thought I was crazy."

I'd heard this a lot with people who die and come back having a new heightened sense of awareness. Some can suddenly see dead people. Others become highly intuitive. A woman with blonde hair and soft skin took the microphone after Brian.

"I am from Peru, so forgiving please of my accent," she said in broken English. "I have near-death experience. It taught me that we all have ability to calm our heart. It's breathing into the heart—like a baby. Babies teach us this. We can all get there. We just have to take a moment to get there." She stopped herself as her eyes welled up with tears. "It's so beautiful when you find this peaceful heart."

Diane took the microphone from the woman and said, "You know, one in ten people walking around the U.S. has had a near-death experience. One in ten. That's about twenty-five million people. That's pretty extraordinary."

Eventually Deana, the featured speaker, got up to talk. She was round, crass, and full of charm. She talked about how she had died twice—each during standard operations.

Geez! I hope she switched doctors.

"The first time I saw the *Light*, I was on the operating table," she said. "It's as if I floated above my body and was looking down on the whole thing. I heard the doctor and the nurse making comments about somebody's shoes. It was really wild, considering I was *dead*, and there they were talking about footwear!"

Deana's "take it or leave it" delivery was hilarious.

"I told the doctors what I heard them say after I woke from the operation, and they couldn't believe it," she laughed.

"You were out," the doctor insisted. "There's no way you could have heard any conversations."

"Sorry to disappoint you, but I heard everything you said."

After she watched the doctors and nurses, she found herself walking down a tunnel.

"The best way I can describe it is like being on one of those walkways in the airport," she said. "You're walking, but you're going faster than you normally would. I got to the *Light*, and it was like Dorothy in *The Wizard of Oz* going from black and white to color when she steps into Oz. It was brilliant," she said, holding out her hands as if she were reliving the moment. "I could *hear* the grass moving. I could *see* the textures of the flowers. It was excruciatingly beautiful."

She said that she tried to enter the *Light* by crossing a bridge, and there were three beings in her way that wouldn't allow her in.

"And with that negative thought that I couldn't enter, I was suddenly back on the operating table and in my body."

The second time she saw the *Light* was years later. Her husband had unfortunately passed away in a car crash, and a few days after the accident, she had to go into the hospital for another routine procedure.

"I was so devastated that I decided I was going to go be with my husband," she explained. "I didn't want to be here without him."

So she got her will and all of her paperwork in order before going under the knife.

"And you don't understand," she said. "I *hate* paperwork more than anything in the world, so this was really a pain in the ass for me."

During the operation, she went under and immediately saw her husband.

"I walked up to him with my arms open, and I said, 'I'm here to be with you,' and he put out his hand to stop me and said, 'No. It's not your time.' And I looked at him like he was nuts and said, 'Do you know how much paperwork I had to do to *get* here?' He looked at me and said, 'It's not up to me, or even you. It's just not your time. You haven't had enough life experiences yet. You haven't lived enough, hurt enough, shared enough. When it's your time to go, I will come and get you.'"

So Deana went back to her life as a massage therapist, where she tells people about their past lives.

"We've all been everything," she explained. "We take on a body over and over again to learn all the lessons that body can teach us."

Try doing it 541 times. I'm pooped.

Two days later, I went to Diane's house for my session with Deana.

"You two can head upstairs," Diane said.

We walked up to the room where Deana was doing her readings. I had no idea if I was getting massaged or if she was just going to talk.

"Is it okay if I record the session?" I asked, holding out my digital recorder.

"Oh, of course." She smiled. "Go ahead and sit on the futon and take off your shoes and socks."

I sat on the futon as Deana slowly made her way to the floor.

"I'm not as flexible as I used to be," she joked, as she tried to bend down.

As she got settled, she reached for my left foot.

"Tell me your name again?"

"I'm Jenniffer," I said.

While Deana could have easily gotten my information and bio from Diane, I had a feeling she wasn't the type who cared one way or the other about doing research on her subjects. She wasn't selling a book and rarely did these sessions. She was just gonna rub my feet and tell me some stories.

"All you need to do is relax," she said, starting to rub my left foot. "I'm going to ask for some truth and light and healing."

Great. Just promise me you'll keep doing the rubbing part . . .

Deana looked over my right shoulder.

"Your guide says her name is Cynthia and that she's been with you since the beginning. Oh, and you have two others, Roger and—what's your name?" she asked the air. "Howard. Okay."

Cynthia, Roger, and Howard? I guess that's better than Moe, Larry, and Curly.

"They say you have to take some time for you. And not only that; you can't fix anybody but you. They are concerned about that. You keep trying to do more *out there*, instead of doing more *in here*," she said, putting her hand on her chest.

She rubbed and looked, like she was waiting for a transmission.

"Okay, the first life I see is of you as a doctor. It's during the time just after Henry VIII. I see an apothecary jar full of leeches that you take with you to bleed people. You treated some very impressive folks. You really didn't think that cutting and putting people's arms in water was the way to heal, but it was what everyone practiced at the time. You were interested in herbs, unlike some of the other doctors, but you had to keep it sort of hidden because you didn't want anyone to doubt your abilities or accuse you of witchcraft. But you could see that the herbs worked. You had to be very diplomatic about who you shared this information with. This is relevant in this lifetime because you seem to be able to read people very well when deciding *who* you share *what* with. You learned this in this lifetime as a doctor."

This was interesting to me. Switching gears from "journalist" to "spiritual warrior," I quickly realized I couldn't shout from the tree-tops that I was doing things like going to sit in a session to learn about my past lives. "Healing with herbs" really applied to my life now. I still get flack for treating my child's reflux with chamomile tea instead of Prevacid. Deana was also right about being careful when sharing information. My entire life I've had to "pick my audience," so to speak.

Deana went on to list a variety of lifetimes. She saw me in ancient Greece as an athlete, Tibet as a monk, Europe as a nun and a priest.

"You have been enough monks, priests, and nuns in enough different religions to know that they are *all* correct, and they are *all* wrong," she laughed. "All this dogma in religions, it was created by man and not God. What matters is that you do the best you can every day and not to judge."

This seemed to be a theme for me.

"We need to be the best we can be and then we have no regrets at the end of our lives. But nobody's 'best' is the same. One person's 'best' might be to run for president and another's might be to sit on the couch and pet their dog. And if we don't beat ourselves up over it, it helps."

I laughed at the thought of my family "celebrating" someone who sat on the couch to pet the dog. While my dad *loved* dogs, an impressive résumé was much more important.

"God does not build one taller than another. We do, however, all come with our own unique experiences," she said.

Deana looked up again at where she said my "guides" were standing.

"They're telling me you get your best thoughts when you run," she said. Interestingly, I hadn't mentioned that I was a runner, and I was in jeans and a sweatshirt, so it's not like she could see that I was in shape. "Some people meditate, but you can't sit still, and get the same benefits from a good run."

I'd tried for years to meditate, but she was absolutely spot on— sitting still in silence for me lasted about three minutes before I'd give up and go *do* something.

She continued to push on the pressure points of my feet.

"Am I hurting you?" she asked.

"Not in the slightest," I said. I'm one of those people who tells the massage therapist to push as hard as they can so I can feel the burn. I was really enjoying the foot massage, and things got even better when I heard piano music coming through the walls.

"Ahhhh, thank you, Diane," Deana said. Diane was a Julliard-trained musician and played several instruments. "That piece is called 'The Sigh.' She was playing it yesterday."

As the music floated through the air, I got goose bumps. "Sorry about that, I have been getting goose bumps so much lately," I said, as Deana rubbed my calves. "Now it's *really* obvious that I didn't shave my legs."

"Oh, I don't care," she laughed. "When you hear stuff that is your *real truth*, you get what is called 'confirmation chills.' Your body gives them to you to catch your attention. It's saying, 'Pay attention. This is real. This is truth. Be present now.'"

She kept rubbing my legs as the chills subsided. She stared off to the side, waiting for more information. Deana's eyes lit up as if she was looking at something hilarious.

"I see you as a baker in the Loire Valley in France. You owned a pastry shop and baked breads and cakes, and you were just lovely and funny." She laughed. "Your husband in your current lifetime owned a pub across the street back then, and you were great friends."

While I can't bake a cake to save my life, both my husband and I are obsessed with the Loire Valley. We've often talked about taking our dream vacation in that region. Yet we've never been there before.

"You recognized your husband right away when you met him in this lifetime, didn't you?"

"You're right," I said.

When I met Clay, we were both struggling traffic reporters in our twenties. I was sitting at the computer typing in some travel times. He walked behind me and squeezed my shoulder to say hello. I got "confirmation chills" throughout my entire body.

"Let's see how you died in that baker lifetime," she said, looking to the side.

"Yes, let's," I smiled, enjoying my foot rub.

"Oh, there was a terrible fire, and you tripped and fell and succumbed to the smoke."

Bummer.

"You were gone from your body before you burned completely," she said.

"Well, that's nice to know."

"Sometimes when we get close to death, it's almost like we get scared out of our bodies. The spirit leaves, and then the body goes ahead. This is big with plane crashes, where the spirits will vacate the body before impact."

Deana reached for my right hand and started rubbing.

"In your lifetime just before the one you have now, you were born in 1935. You were male and wanted to serve in the army. You went to Korea. You were injured and came home. You were so disillusioned when you came back because you couldn't understand all the death and killing. You wondered how religion could say not to kill anybody, yet here you were assigned to do this."

I've always been disgusted by war. The injustice of people dying over disagreements has never sat well with me.

"So you went to several different churches to try and find one that worked for you. You never found one that satisfied you entirely."

Here we go again.

"You kept saying, 'There's gotta be more out there because I'm still hungry,'" she said, pushing into my palm. "You died in a car accident in 1965."

"Oh no," I said. "I was only thirty?"

"The brakes went out and the car went over a cliff," she said, in a sort of deal-with-it tone. "That was that."

Deana rubbed a few more seconds and then took her hands away from mine.

"I think we're done," she said. No more lives. No more rubs.

"Oh wow," I said, surprised that our time was already up.

"Do you have any questions?" she asked with a smile.

"Well yes, actually," I said, putting my shoes back on. "When you saw the *Light*, did you feel totally at peace?"

"Oh God, yes! There's something about the peace that comes from harmony. That thing that goes 'yes . . . so *that's* how it all fits together!' When we can find a beautiful piece of music that gives us those confirmation chills, or even great sex. We can't have it all the time, but once in a while, it helps us understand, *that's* what we're looking for. Because when we are in the *Light*, it feels like that *all* the time."

I'd always been pretty scared to die. But hearing that it's like having lots of "great sex" made it seem a lot less intimidating.

KNOCK, KNOCK, KNOCK.

"Oh no," I said, not wanting my conversation to be over.

A man poked his head into the room. Deana's next appointment had arrived. It was time for me to go.

When I got home, Clay was making chocolate chip cookies from scratch.

"So?" he asked, as he turned on the mixer.

"I was a baker in the Loire Valley, and you owned a bar across the street," I said, dipping my finger in the batter. "I'm thinking maybe she had our roles mixed up."

I wondered how many other couples on the planet ever had a conversation like this while standing in the kitchen. My guess—maybe two.

"Did you get a massage out of the deal?" he asked.

"A foot and hand rub," I said.

"Well that's something!"

beware of preachers with mullets

Develop Your Intuition

Cornerstone Baptist Church sign:

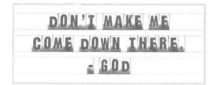

DON'T MAKE ME
COME DOWN THERE.
– GOD

I WONDER how Millard is doing?

I was brushing my teeth one morning, and Millard Fuller popped into my head out of nowhere. I hadn't thought about him since I was in San Diego at the conference where he was the keynote speaker. I pulled out my BlackBerry and emailed Bettie Youngs, the author of Millard's biography.

"How are things coming with the screenplay for Millard's life story?" I wrote.

Within minutes, Bettie sent me Millard's obituary.

"Oh my GOD!" I screamed. Millard had just died from complications of a brief illness. He was seventy-four years old. I called Therese right away. "I was thinking of him as I was brushing my teeth and now he's dead. I'm so sad."

While I barely knew Millard, he was one of those people who truly changed my life with one simple encounter. He made me want to serve people. I couldn't believe he was gone.

"Your intuition is really growing," she said. "It's like a muscle—the more you use it, the stronger it gets."

As I WASHED dishes several weeks later, I got a picture in my head of an old acquaintance of mine named Randy Rogers. Randy owned a company that ran video shoots for press junkets. I hadn't thought about him or seen him since the late 1990s, back when I used to do movie reviews for television.

Why is he coming to my mind right now?

There was one junket in particular during which Randy and I bonded over our newly discovered spiritual journeys. We were both skeptical journalists going into all of this. He started as an award-winning photojournalist and wound up running his own production company in Hollywood. I was a news reporter who had been switched to the "celebrity beat" in L.A. and New York. I had just done my first interview with James Van Praagh, and was telling Randy how he supposedly brought through my dead grandmother. Randy had just gone to see an acupuncturist who told him about some of his past lives.

"I thought *acupuncture* was bizarre, okay—so to tell me I have *past lives?* I thought the whole thing sounded nuts," he explained. We spent three hours comparing notes on our experiences.

I hadn't seen him in more than ten years.

"I wonder what Randy is up to?" I thought as I rinsed some plates. Then I remembered the Millard incident. "Oh *shit.* I hope he's not *dead!*"

The very next day, I was driving to work, and my cell phone rang.

"Hey Jen, it's Sara," the voice on the other end said. Sara had been my publicist for my first book. "I have an author coming through

Chicago, and I was hoping you could do an article on him for your blog. His name is Randall Rogers."

"That's funny, but I was just thinking of a friend of mine with a similar name," I said. I didn't think it could be the same guy, because Randy never mentioned being a writer.

When I got to my desk, I opened the press release from Sara, and was amazed to find that "Randall" was the same Randy that I'd known years before.

"Of course I'll do a piece," I said to Sara.

When Randy and I connected on the phone, it was as if no time had passed since our last conversation. He shared with me several "coincidences" that he now believed to be something much deeper. It all started with a vivid dream he had about a former classmate named Kathy, whom he discovered had died from cancer. Randy now got *intuitive hits* from Kathy, and felt more tapped in to his spiritual side than ever before. He'd put all of his experiences into a book called *The Key of Life* that he was promoting across the country.

"Kathy comes to me a lot," he said. "During one of my dreams, she told me about where she was. She said if you looked at a glass filled with water and ice, you are the ice cubes and those on the Other Side are the water in between each cube. We are still connected, but just in a different form."

I loved that analogy. My other favorite comes from my friend Denise Guzzardo, a psychic and medium I featured in my first book.

"It's like tuning in to a radio station," she said. "Sometimes it's clear and sometimes it's fuzzy, but they're so close. Just on a different channel."

"I'm so glad Sara called me," I said. "It's so nice to be able to talk about this stuff with someone who doesn't think I'm crazy."

"The more you tap in to it, the more often it happens," Randy said. "I was as scientific as it gets before all this stuff happened to me. It's all just matching vibrations. I mean really, there are no coincidences."

"I wish you could have seen my one-woman show," I said. "It just closed, but I talked about all of this in my play."

"Will you do another run?"

"I've been thinking about it."

ON THE day of my last performance, I was anxious to take a hiatus. I'd done about fifty shows in three back-to-back stretches, so I was ready to stop talking for a while.

As I stood on the stage to take a bow, I saw four people in the front row giving me a standing ovation. I figured I must have known them because they were as vocal and responsive as my family or friends. But as I took a closer look, nobody was familiar. I saw a father who might have been in his fifties and three young adults, all who looked to be in their early twenties.

"Hi," I said to the man after the clapping died down. "How did you hear about the show?"

"I work with Clare, and she gave me your book," he said.

Clare was the woman who got her dream job working for the girls in Guatemala after she started *changing her vocabulary*. I quickly remembered that she'd sent me an email earlier that week telling me her friend Greg and his family would be in the audience for my final show. She described him as "one of the most generous men I know."

"All of my kids read your book, too," Greg said with a huge smile, pointing to the three standing next to him.

"We can really relate," one of his daughters added.

"Really?" I said. "How so?"

Apparently, all three of Greg's kids can either see dead people or have an intuition that goes deeper than most.

"Really?" I gasped. Greg is a trader with the Chicago Board of Trade. I couldn't imagine the subject of his kids seeing dead people being a hot topic on his lunch break. "And how's that workin' for ya?" I joked.

"It's been, uh ... well, interesting to say the least," he said with a laugh.

After talking to his children for a while, I exchanged information with one of the daughters, Elizabeth. She had beautiful red hair and deep brown eyes.

"We really need to go to lunch," she said. "I'd like to tell you some of my stories."

A couple weeks later, I made plans to meet Elizabeth at the Salt and Pepper Diner in the Lincoln Park neighborhood of Chicago. When we sat down, she told me that while in college a couple of years prior, she was in a terrible car accident and lost her best friend Sam in the tragedy. She doesn't remember anything for nine full hours after the accident, but she did have a vivid "dream," as she called it, of an adventure she took with Sam.

"Maybe you were technically dead, and you were with him in Heaven?" I suggested. "Do you think the accident brought about some intuition you didn't have before?"

"I've always had it," she explained. "Since we were all kids. My sister actually sees dead people. For me, it's more hunches or even dreams that reveal information I might need to know down the road. My brother is the youngest, and he has it more than any of us."

Elizabeth then went on to tell me how she babysat for kids with similar gifts.

"Their parents chalk it up to having 'imaginary friends,'" she said. "They'll feed them diet soda and crappy food, and those are like poisons to intuitive kids. They have no clue how gifted their children are. It breaks my heart."

"How did your parents take all this when you were growing up?" I asked.

"They were amazing. We had nuns in our Catholic schools who

wanted to medicate us because we were done with our homework too fast and bored in class. My dad told them to forget it and moved us to a different school."

"You are so lucky. There are so many people out there who think this is a curse or just hope it will go away." I thought of my high-school friend James or the fireman who said he saw and heard spirits.

"I know," she said, throwing her hands up. "*We're* the normal ones!"

As Elizabeth and I kept talking, I saw through the glass window a woman walk by who looked a lot like Therese. I banged on the glass and got her attention.

"Hey!" I said, as I waved her in. "That's Therese Rowley."

"The medium from your book and your play?" Elizabeth asked. "No *way!*"

Therese lived around the corner. I had invited her to join us for lunch, but she had a dentist appointment. Apparently, she got out early.

"Hey, you!" she said, taking a seat. "How are we doing?"

Therese only knew that Elizabeth had come to see my play with her family—nothing more.

"Elizabeth is intuitively gifted," I said. "She and her sister and brother are all like you," I laughed. "And the good news is, her parents were totally on board with everything when she was growing up."

"Wow, you are very blessed," Therese said.

As Therese and Elizabeth talked, Elizabeth mentioned that her sister was not sure how to handle the ghosts she kept seeing in her apartment.

"They walk around, and she's like 'I don't know who you are or why you are here, so I wish you would go away,'" Elizabeth said.

"Well, she can set boundaries with those spirits," Therese said, as if this was a totally normal conversation. "She could just say to them, 'I only have time to talk to you all at 5:00 p.m. on Tuesdays, so do *not* come back until that time.' You just have to lay down some ground rules."

Who knew?

"I really want my sister to come and see you," Elizabeth said. "This would help her so much."

"I was thinking I should hold some workshops on this, and maybe some for parents of gifted kids, too," Therese said. "I'm writing a manual for parents and kids with intuitive gifts."

"I know so many people who would buy that book," Elizabeth said.

"If I were given drugs when I was a kid, I never would have been able to identify my gifts and use them to help others. We have to create another path for these kids so they can know they are gifted and not disordered. Then they can develop their intuitive skills." Therese's enthusiasm started oozing out of her pores. And then, as if someone just plopped down onto the booth next to Elizabeth, Therese started squinting and looking to the side.

"This usually means a spirit is here," I said to Elizabeth, figuring if anyone could handle that kind of bizarre information, it would be a woman with similar talents.

Therese exhaled three times quickly.

"Is it Sam?" I asked.

"Yes," Therese said, pointing to Elizabeth. "I'm seeing him get ejected from the car. I can see him get thrown ...'" Therese put her hands on her throat, as if she was *feeling* the impact of the accident.

Elizabeth looked shocked.

"He's with you a lot," Therese said. "You have to tell his story and your story of your time together. That was Heaven. You were with him in Heaven. This will help others. He's showing me how he's going to help you along with this." Therese then started laughing. "He is such a lively spirit."

I watched Elizabeth listen to Therese. She seemed to be having a hard time processing this whole exchange. And then her eyes started to well up as she tried to speak.

"I wrote it all out," Elizabeth said. "It was my thesis in college. It just came to me. I knew it was true. It felt like it was exactly what had happened, even though I don't have any real memories of what happened."

"Yes, you do," Therese said. "Sam helped you remember."

WITHIN THE next few months, Elizabeth asked me to help produce a video for a charity called the H.E.A.R. Foundation that her father helped start.

"We're going to be giving out food to underprivileged families on the South Side of Chicago," she explained. "Can you help us?"

"I'd love to!" I said.

The morning of the shoot, my mother came by for her weekly visit.

"I want you to turn on channel 10 right now," she said.

"Why?" I was almost afraid to ask.

"I don't want you to judge, Jenniffer," she scolded. "His name is Joel Osteen, and he's a very spiritual speaker."

I turned on the television and saw a guy with a mullet and big teeth preaching to a stadium full of followers in Houston about the "Word of the Lord."

"Mom, this is a televangelist!" I screamed.

"He's different," she barked. "He's not like the others. He doesn't ask for money. He speaks from the heart. Just give him a chance!"

I tried to give him a chance, but the crawl on the bottom of the screen quickly distracted me.

"Mom, when they flash 'join our community' on the screen every three seconds, that's asking for money," I said.

"Just listen!" she insisted.

"You can*not* be contained," Osteen was saying in a southern drawl. "Some of you will be bestselling authors or screenwriters or run your own businesses. You just don't know what God has in store for you. He believes in you."

The crowd clapped and held up their Bibles.

"It sounds like he is saying that to be successful you need to become a bestselling author or own a business," I said. "What if you are a security guard or work at Burger King? Will God not love you as much?" I asked.

"That is *not* what he is saying," she snapped. She shook her head in disappointment. "He wants you to aim high. He is saying that anyone can reach for whatever they want."

I had a real problem with the whole "entitlement" craze that came from the release of *The Secret.* Suddenly, people thought that if they just created a vision board, everything would be okay once they got all that *stuff.*

"It's not about your title or getting rich, Mom. Some people don't want to run a company. And if you *do* run a company, does that mean you're automatically going to be happy?" I knew a lot of really rich and successful people who were completely miserable.

"He is encouraging people to follow their dreams," she said.

"You need to feel God's love and know that he supports you to succeed," Joel continued.

"It's his delivery that bugs me," I said.

Any time I hear that "fire and brimstone" lilt in a speaker's voice, accompanied by the big hand wave, I just zone out. "I don't want my spirituality to be spoken in *vibrato.*"

"You're so judgmental," Mom said. "You claim to be spiritual, but you judge all the time."

"I'm sure Joel Osteen had a lovely message. He's obviously doing something right to fill stadiums, but he just isn't for me," I sighed. "Everyone has a different way of getting there, Mom."

An hour later, it was time for me to head to my video shoot.

"Do you want me to go for you instead?" Clay asked. I had been writing all week, and the thought of having Clay take my place was pretty appealing.

"Hmmm," I said. "It's tempting."

I stood by the front door for a moment, and as I reached down to pick up the camera case, I heard:

You need to go to this shoot. There's someone you're supposed to meet.

"Okay," I said.

"Okay, what?" Clay asked.

"I'm supposed to go," I said. "I just got an *intuitive hit.*"

"Riiiiight," Clay said, as he walked back into the kitchen.

As I was headed downtown to pick up my cameraman, I pulled into the express lanes on the highway, which were wide open. Since there was nobody on the road, I took the left lane and turned on my radio. Within a couple of minutes, I noticed a small white car riding my bumper. I looked in the rearview mirror and saw a middle-aged man honking his horn as he got nervously close to my car.

I looked down at my speedometer. I was going 65.

"Okay, buddy," I said, as I changed lanes. "You win the race. Go ahead."

I moved to the right lane, and this man rode next to me so he could flip me off and honk a few more times. I was trying not to laugh because it was so ridiculous. I was out of his way. He could go on with his day. But noooooo. He just wanted to be angry with somebody, I guess, because he stayed there for what felt like an eternity.

And then, I saw something white out of the corner of my eye. I looked to my left, inside the man's car. He was holding up a sign that read: LEFT LANE LAW.

It took me a minute to realize what I was seeing. This was a homemade sign. He actually sat in his house, scrounged up some poster board, got a big ass marker, and created something that he could keep in his car as he drove around the city. His hope was to then find a person going the speed limit or slower in the left lane, so he could remind them of the dreaded LEFT LANE LAW and show off his workmanship.

What a colossal waste of energy.

I thought about joining in on the "honking and flipping off" party, but then I remembered Deepak Chopra's words about "being right." Anger is anger. It still causes your blood to boil and raises your heart rate, even if you believe that your stance is the correct one.

I took several deep breaths and tried to get centered, my hand quivering with the desire to extend my middle finger.

This is so fucking hard!

It took incredible patience *not* to react to this guy, but, eventually, he drove away. My pulse went back to normal in a matter of minutes. But I had a hard time getting his furious face out of my head.

I wonder if he has more signs in his backseat? Perhaps a "STOP SIGN LAW" or "PICK UP AFTER YOUR DOG" poster?

When I arrived at the shoot, I saw a gigantic U-Haul truck unloading pounds of frozen poultry. Various smaller vans and trucks were spread out around the area from different churches and Catholic leagues, and dozens of volunteers were loading and unloading at the same time.

"This is incredible," I said, looking at all the food.

"Hey, Jen," I heard a voice say. Elizabeth walked over and gave me a hug. Her dad quickly followed.

"I am so impressed," I said to Greg.

"It feels good to help," he said.

I interviewed the organizers and some of the volunteers. I watched mothers with ripped jackets and no winter gloves bring grocery carts full of kids in hopes of also filling those carts with food. There was a man talking to Greg who just *oozed* grace. His name was Pastor Dan Johnson, and he was there to collect some food for his struggling community.

"We have to rehabilitate these kids," he explained to Greg. "It's not about locking them up like they do with prisons. We need to teach them skills and tell them we believe in them. I learned business on the streets when I was nine. I am a product of the streets. Now I take kids who are going to be suspended, and I tell the schools, 'You give them to me, and I'll work with them. I'll put them to work and help them find their passion.' We've done that with six hundred kids so far. They beg to come to our programs now." He smiled.

"Why doesn't the media know about you?" I asked.

"Oh, this isn't about getting exposure," he said. "This is about changing lives. I see plenty of preachers, and they care more about being on television than they do about getting their hands dirty. I just want to focus on these kids."

I had started my day being less than impressed listening to Joel Osteen preach to more than fifty thousand people in a stadium. Now I stood in front of a pastor who maybe helps a few hundred people a year, and he made me want to be a better person.

My intuitive hit was right. I *was* supposed to go to this shoot.

A COUPLE weeks after that video shoot, I started feeling extreme pain in my mouth.

"Go to the dentist," Clay said.

"We don't have dental coverage," I said, making excuses.

After a while, however, I couldn't ignore the shooting pain on the left side of my face, so I caved in and made an appointment.

Five words I never expected to hear in my thirties: *You need a root canal*. For some reason, I figured this was a procedure that happens for really *old* people. Apparently not.

Spiritually speaking, teeth are supposed to be our antennae. I can't remember where I heard this theory initially, but my friend Cindy, whose father was a dentist, said that when we are getting work done on our mouths, it's a spiritual upgrade. Sounded good to me.

The morning of my procedure, I was particularly tense. I hate needles and anything that involves drills in my mouth. So I started yapping at the ceiling.

Please Dad, don't let this hurt too much. And if I'm not supposed to get this procedure, you better show me a sign pronto, because my appointment is in an hour.

As I was getting ready to leave, Britt started looking needy.

"Orange cement truck?" he asked.

We scoured the first floor for this damn truck to the point where I was opening drawers I hadn't opened in years just to say I'd tried everything. I didn't find the truck, so I quickly distracted my son with a fresh bowl of blueberries.

"Boo-babies!" he said, dipping his hand in the bowl.

One thing I did find during my search was an old photo from my mom and dad's wedding.

I was in all of my parents' weddings, except the first one—I hadn't been born yet—so it's not uncommon for me to find photos around the house of one of their nuptial ceremonies. There are only two pictures in existence from their first marriage. Mom is eighteen and Dad is twenty. Dad looks terrified, and my mom looks excited. I pulled it out with a smile and placed it on the counter before heading out the door.

When I arrived for my root canal, I got a quick *intuitive hit* that I'm supposed to bring a copy of my book with me.

Why would I bring a book? For the guy doing my root canal? Really?

As confusing as this was, I'd learned that when I got these urges, I'd better listen. Without fail, I'd run into someone who was supposed to have my book for some reason.

Please, Dad, help this go smoothly.

"You're going to feel a little pinch," Dr. Weisbart said, as a needle the size of my forearm went into my mouth.

He started to drill, and then he started to chat. I've always found it amusing that dentists or oral surgeons start asking you questions as they are placing large instruments into your mouth.

"So after you were in here for the consultation, I thought your name looked familiar, so I looked you up and made the connection. I just loved your dad," he said. "How long ago did he die?"

"Mmmmshhh ayyyyyttt yeeeearz agggggho," I mumbled.

"One of my good friends also died from a brain tumor in his fifties," he continued. "My dad died fifteen years ago, and my mom says she talks to him all the time, like she's having a phone conversation with him or something." He laughed like this notion was crazy. "But you tried to talk to your dad on the Other Side, right?"

I tried to answer as he continued to drill. My lips felt like they were stretched out to Peoria.

"I'm very interested in your book," he said. "I normally only read mysteries and thrillers, but I'm really curious to read yours. It comes at a good time for me."

Funny you should mention that book.

I pointed to the window where I'd placed my purse and gestured to the book I now knew was for him.

"Mmmmm hmmmm, therrrrgh lggggkkkk dahhhhh," I groaned.

"Wow! You brought me one?! I will start reading it right away," he said, delighted.

As I sat through the procedure, which I'm happy to report was surprisingly less painful than expected, I noticed that every single song coming through the speakers was one that reminded me of Dad—whether it was something he played on the keyboards with his band or a personal favorite he liked to play at home. There were so many in a row, it was almost comical. The fears that started my day were now a distant memory.

I tried to wipe the drool from my chin as I stumbled to the counter to pay. I turned on my BlackBerry and listened to my messages. There was only one.

"Hi, honey. It's your mom. So today, your father and I would have been married forty-three years. Of course, if we had stayed together, I probably would have killed him long before he became ill, but I always remember our anniversary. Hope your day is going well. I'm *soooo* proud of you."

Since the novocaine prevented me from speaking clearly, I decided to send her a quick email.

Dear Mom,

Dad already told me it was your anniversary this morning before I left the house. He was with me at my root canal too. I'll fill you in later.

Love, Me

When I got home and started blogging about all of this, the phone rang. It was the bank.

"We're calling about your order for checks for the Tim Weigel Scholarship Fund," the voice said. We had started a scholarship fund in Dad's name to help people in financial need pay for furthering their education. I hadn't marked a size preference when I had ordered the checks several weeks before.

What are the chances that they would call right now?

Later that night, I had dinner with my skeptical friend Jim. He thinks everything that I experience is just a bizarre coincidence, and rolls his eyes whenever I start up with my "I get signs from the dead" talk.

"You know that means nothing," he said.

"Let's recap," I said. "I started my day finding that wedding picture. The guy brings up my dead dad. Every song they played was Dad's favorite song, then my mom left me a message about their anniversary, and the bank calls about the Weigel Fund? And you think *all* of it is a coincidence?"

"Lucky coincidence," he insisted.

"You know, you should try to be more positive," I said, sipping my wine. "Just open your mind to the possibility that we don't know everything that's going on."

"Okay," Jim said. "I'm *positive* that it's a coincidence."

"Well I'm *positive* that we're somehow all connected," I said. "And it's a lot more fun having my perspective than yours."

ONE DAY as the holiday months approached, I was on the phone with my brother.

"I think this baby is coming early," he said. His firstborn son was due November nineteenth. "I just have a feeling it's going to be sooner."

"Let me ask Britt," I joked. Since it was known in the family that my son liked talking to his dead grandpa, I figured I'd test his intuitive skills, too.

"Britt, are Rafer and Tiffany going to have a baby this week?" I asked. He was playing with a truck on the floor.

"Nope," he said, not hesitating for a second or looking up from his toy.

"Is the baby coming next week?"

"Nope," he repeated, still not looking up.

"What about the following week?" I asked. This would have been the week the baby was due.

"Yes," he said. "On Friday."

Rafer heard my conversation through the phone.

"I hope he's wrong!" he moaned. "That would be *after* the due date. He's due on a Thursday."

The week before Thanksgiving, I was on the phone with Rafer again.

"If the baby doesn't show up by Thursday, we induce Thursday night," he said.

"Okay," I said. I looked over at Britt as he ate his mac and cheese. "Is the baby coming this Thursday, Britt?" He rolled his eyes as if he was tired of answering this question.

"No Momma, *Friday*," he said.

The next night, I went to dinner with my friend Jacquey. She was seven months pregnant with her first child, and we hadn't seen each other in a couple of years. Jacquey now lived in Los Angeles, but we met back in our twenties when we were doing a children's musical for Second City.

"Can you believe Rafer is having a baby any day now?" I said.

"See," she laughed. "We *all* shift our priorities when we get older."

"So what made you change your mind about having kids? You were so dead set against it."

"I just sort of switched my focus," she said. "I mean, I looked back on the last few years, and all the auditions and the uncertainty. It was sort of like, 'Well, what do I have to show for my life? A bunch of auditions or a family?' Family and my relationships seemed like the much better choice."

"Isn't it amazing how self-centered we were in our twenties?"

Jacquey put her hands on her perfectly round belly. She looked radiant as a mom-to-be.

"I was always comparing myself to the person next to me or wondering if I could do more," she said, shaking her head. "I remember waking up in the middle of the night in a total panic worrying about what I *wasn't*. I don't think I ever truly enjoyed who I *was*."

THURSDAY THE nineteenth came and went, and there was still no word from Rafer about his baby. So Friday morning, the inducing began. All day, I was furiously texting him for updates, but nothing was happening.

"Tiffany is still eight centimeters, but no pushing yet," he reported.

"I have a book signing tonight, so I hope it happens before then," I wrote. "I don't want to miss it!"

Therese and I were doing a talk at Burke's Books in Park Ridge. Burke's is where I was headed when I got the call that Rafer had been hired by CNN, right after my first book came out. On that night, I was lost, depressed, and feeling sorry for myself. While I certainly didn't have all the answers in time for my second visit, I now knew that my stories inspired people. I didn't have a set income yet, but I *did* have a lot more trust pumping through my veins.

"They are expecting a full house," I told Therese, as I read an email from Pat, the owner of Burke's. "It's only because you are joining me," I said.

"Oh *please*," she said. "I'm *so* riding on your coattails, Thelma."

We joke that we're like the Thelma and Louise of spirituality (only without that whole *drive your car off the cliff* ending).

"Guess what else," Therese said.

"What?"

"I think I got a book deal," she said. "Can you believe it?"

"That's great! Congratulations."

As I made my way to Park Ridge, it was a clear night, almost fifty degrees, and I knew *exactly* where I was going. No snowstorm. No crying fit. No Therese talking me off of the ledge. All I needed **now** was a call from my brother . . .

BEEEEEEEP.

My BlackBerry suddenly went off. I was one block away **from** Burke's. I pulled up to the store just as Therese pulled up **on the** other side of the road. I looked down at the message from **my** brother. Heathcliff John Weigel had entered the world. (Tiffany's favorite book is *Wuthering Heights*, in case you were wondering.)

I called Rafer just before I entered the store. I could hear in **his** voice that he was beaming.

"I've been up all night, but it was amazing. He's beautiful," he **said.** He sounded exhausted. "Britt was right. He did come Friday."

Rather than calling to celebrate a job, he was announcing **that a** new life was unfolding.

"I'm an aunt!" I told everyone at Burke's Books.

Everything else seemed so irrelevant.

THE NEXT morning, I was about to leave the house for a run, **but** I decided to take a walk instead. The fall colors were in full **bloom,** and I wanted to soak in the smells and sights.

I took some deep breaths and tried to let out all my stress **with** each exhale.

"Visualize the white light going into your lungs and being dis-tributed into your blood." I remembered the words from one of **my** Master John CDs. "Visualize yourself glowing in the peace and be-ing of divine love."

The forest preserve was a few blocks from my house, and **soon** after I entered, I heard leaves crunching. Something was **headed** toward me. I looked to my right and saw the most beautiful **baby** deer. It was not even ten feet away, staring right at me, with **giant** brown eyes and a white tail wagging behind.

I stopped cold in my tracks, blown away by its beauty. I'd **never** been so close to a deer, let alone one that was practically smiling at me. If I had been running with my iPod, I would have blown right past without looking back. Because I chose to walk and smell the air, I was able to appreciate everything around me.

"Hi, you perfect thing," I whispered. She didn't run, but kept looking right in my eyes.

As I stared back, I was overwhelmed with a feeling of calm. I could have been there to kill her for all she knew, and yet she was standing in front of me, without fear, enjoying the moment. I wanted to *become* her—trusting and beautiful, even when facing uncertainty. I suddenly got this *knowing* that everything was going to be okay. Truly. I didn't need to worry. Just like this deer, I too would be safe and protected.

None of this nonsense matters, Jen.

The deer blinked a few times as her white tail whipped back and forth. I was afraid to breathe for fear that it would scare her away. I felt total bliss. Then, the bliss turned to tears.

"Thank you," I whispered, my chest heaving with a cleansing cry. "Thank you."

When I got home from my walk, I sat in my backyard. I listened to the leaves blow with the wind and inhaled the Indian summer air. It was fresh and familiar. I leaned back in the chair and looked up at the sky. The yellow and orange leaves lingered overhead like a gorgeous painting. For the first time in a while, I could feel my life.

Don't run too fast, Jen. You might miss something beautiful.

you are enough

Always Do Your Best

Glad Tidings Assembly Church of God sign:

DON'T BE SO
OPEN MINDED.
YOUR BRAINS MIGHT
FALL OUT.

"HEY, JEN, it's Susan," my voice-over agent said. "I need to check your availability for Bonefish Grill."

"Yahoo!" I yelled up the stairs to Clay. "I got another Bonefish!"

"Thank you, Universe," he yelled back.

This was a radio spot for a national restaurant chain.

"Mommy, no phone." My son was giving me a glare as I held my BlackBerry. "Come here," he said, patting the area by the couch next to him.

One of my biggest pet peeves growing up with my dad was that he always seemed distracted. Every time we would have a conversation at dinner, he would look over my head and half listen to what I was saying. I vowed that I would not be like him when I became a parent. However, I was also a BlackBerry addict.

Always do your best.

This was another one of don Miguel Ruiz's Four Agreements, and it was particularly tough for me to follow. Whether you are washing the dishes or singing on stage, he feels that you should give that task your complete focus and attention by *always doing your best*. In other words, *no* multitasking allowed.

I sat down with Britt on the couch. I heard my BlackBerry vibrate several times. It was out of reach, so I couldn't sneak a peek. Curious George was on television. I'd seen this episode seventy-five times. I find it nearly impossible to seem enthused after multiple viewings of the same cartoon, but I was trying not to let it show.

"George is funny," Britt said, after watching him try to make compost.

The BlackBerry continued to vibrate. Now someone was calling, which made it shake even more.

I hugged Britt close as I tried not to give in to the temptation. Then the landline rang. Nobody called our home phone anymore, so this must have really been important.

"Hold on, sweetie," I said to Britt as I got up. "Hello?"

"We got a speaking gig!" It was Therese, and she was ecstatic.

"Thank you, Universe!" I shouted to the sky.

Therese and I had been asked to do several talks together at the Wilmette Theater, just north of Chicago.

"Can you meet me at Love's Yogurt today at four-thirty so we can get organized?" she asked.

"Sure," I said. "I have a recording session at two, so I'll have plenty of time to get over there."

"See you then."

I ARRIVED at my recording session a few minutes early, so I sat in the waiting room and tried to get centered. Since the Duncan Hines debacle, I had started to doubt my voice-over abilities. It was time to get back in the game.

Thank you, Universe, for helping me do my best.

I remembered a quote from my interview with a medium named Stacy Wells. "Your ability to generate income through your service will come from how you feel about yourself inside —if you're feeling deserving or worthy," she said. "It's all linked to when you are emotionally independent and don't need confirmation *from any outside source.* You want to experience being that source of nurturing to yourself."

I let her words linger in my mind.

My own source of nurturing.

Self-soothing has always been tough for me. I decided that no matter what the people in the recording studio said to me, I was a professional, and I was good enough regardless of their comments.

BZZZZZZZZZZ.

My BlackBerry was vibrating. I looked down, and it was Clay calling.

"Hello?" I whispered, not wanting to draw attention.

"What are you up to?" he asked.

"I'm about to go into this voice-over session, and I'm freaking out."

"Why?"

"Just worried they won't like my delivery."

"No matter what they say it doesn't matter because you're doing your best."

"Thank you. I needed that. I'll call you later."

At that moment, a young guy walked into the waiting area.

"Are you Jenniffer Weigel?" he asked.

Oh yay, he didn't say "Weeeee-gul."

"Yes, I am," I said. We were already off to a good start because he pronounced my name correctly.

I walked into the booth, and he adjusted the microphone to my height. I looked through the glass and saw three other guys sitting there. They each looked to be about thirty.

"Hey, Jenniffer," one of them said. "The copy is right in front of you. We're going to be doing two spots today."

Two spots? Even better!

I was doing a holiday commercial, and the lines were supposed to have a stream of consciousness feel to them.

"Whenever you're ready," the engineer said. "We'll just read them all straight through one at a time, and see where we are."

"Great," I said.

"Here we go, take one," the engineer said.

Always do your best.

The copy was funny. One of my lines was, "I'm on the naughty list." I read through them all, and looked up at the window. The three men looked at each other. They seemed pleased.

"That was awesome," one of them said. "Let's do them again and just switch them up a little bit in the tone just for fun."

"Okay," I said.

"Okay, Bonefish Grill, take two," the engineer said.

I ran through them again. I felt really good about it. I watched the guys all look at each other. One of them leaned in to his "talk" button.

"That was completely perfect," he said. "I think we've got it."

I looked at my watch. I'd been there six minutes.

As I walked out of the session, I called my voice-over agent. The owner of the agency, Linda Jack, answered the phone.

"Hey, Linda, it's Jen Weigel," I said.

"Hey, Jen, shouldn't you be in a session right now?"

"I'm already done."

"That was quick."

"Oh, and it's for two spots and not one. I just wanted to let you know so you could make sure they give you the right paperwork," I said.

"Woo-hoo!" she cheered. "That's a nice holiday gift, huh?"

"Sure is."

Since I had so much time, I decided to treat myself to lunch. Chicago is so gorgeous during the holidays. I walked around Macy's (although to me it will always be Marshall Field's) and looked at the window decorations. There's something about the way the city *smells* during the holiday season that just makes me feel warm and fuzzy inside. From the potpourri in the store to the warm cider sold at the Christmas market, I could barely feel the chill as I maneuvered between the bodies of hundreds of strangers.

I sat on a bench near Daley Plaza and sipped a coffee. There was a bell ringer a few feet from me. He was singing and smiling in twenty-eight-degree temperatures. I watched how he acted with every single customer. Regardless of whether or not they gave him money, he was completely joyful.

"Have a happy holiday, my dear," he said to a woman entering the store, who ignored him.

Talk about always doing your best.

When I walked in to Love's to meet with Therese a bit later, she was smiling from ear to ear.

"So, tell me all the details," I said, as I sat down.

"They said we can talk about anything we want," she said. "I'll bring fliers for the Center for Intuitive Education, and we can hand them out while you sell books in the lobby afterwards. You ready to change some lives, Nellie Bly? We are on our way!"

"That's incredible," I said.

"By the way," Therese said, giving me the once-over. "You look really good."

"I showered," I joked.

"No, I mean energetically. I don't think I've ever seen you so *grounded*."

"I *feel* really good."

"You're shining a whole new light. I'm watching this energy go through you, and it's so beautiful. It's showing me the light that you've been shining your whole life. But you're increasing the frequency of your awareness and your consciousness around love and giving."

I wondered if this had anything to do with all the *Flashdance* buckets I'd been dumping on myself lately.

Therese yawned and cocked her head slightly to the side. I guess I was going to be the recipient of an on-the-spot reading, which was fine with me!

"You are no longer a person who is working on *becoming* known, *becoming* seen, *becoming* understood. You have been understood now by spirit at a level that is so intimate, there's no need to worry about anyone on this planet. The old way of equating your worth by what feedback you get is *done*."

She was right. For so many years, I thought that my job status was what defined me. Now I *knew*, and I mean really felt a *knowing*, that it is my *relationships* that matter most.

Therese blew to the side a couple of times. I looked around. We were the only people in the whole restaurant, so there was nobody to stare at us.

"Okay, your dad is here," she said, looking beside me.

I hadn't *talked* to my dad, through Therese that is, since I met her back in 2001 when I was doing research for my first book. Sure, sometimes I yapped to the air, thinking I was talking to my dad. I felt he gave me signs, and I had that dream where he called me at the bar, but as far as a full-blown "Conversations with Dad from the Other Side"—nada.

"He's showing so much pride and admiration for your spirit and the work you have done on yourself. He says, 'I never would have taken that on!' You passed him up on the spiritual planes," she smiled, as if she had just heard a joke. "He's saying, 'Will you let me into your mansion?' He says the kind of mansions that you are building on a spiritual level outweigh the mansion you were entitled to but did not get in this lifetime. Every time you reach someone's heart and choose the harder road or the humble path, it adds more rooms to that spiritual mansion."

Therese snapped a couple of times and then looked back over to her side.

"He was rich on the outside but poor on the inside; he says you are so rich on the inside, and while it looks like you are poorer on the outside, you are moving into this inner room where these changes get integrated and become your solid core. This *inner* richness will then reflect out to your life. It's from the *inside out*, rather than *outside in*."

Therese pointed to my midsection.

"This is in your third and second chakra—identity and self-esteem—your soul lesson is your ability to see yourself as a fawn—as the doe—your ability to see the beauty, the generosity, and the magnificent heart of the divine mother that you are."

I couldn't believe she'd mentioned the doe. I still thought of her big brown eyes, trusting me completely, whenever I felt lost or worried.

"He's telling me that human journeys are all about gathering the experiences—what it is to make mistakes, feel. It's not about finding a streamline to heaven; it's about getting knocked down and climbing up, as long as you keep your sense of humor."

Therese yawned and cocked her head to the side again.

"I'm seeing Britt. He's showing me Britt. Your dad says, 'All Britt needs right now from you is your hugs. Your presence and your hugs. You can be there for him in a way that I wasn't able to be there for you.'"

I thought about my morning, and how Britt begged me to sit with him. I started to get sad that I'd let him down.

Therese took a few deep breaths and continued.

"He's saying, 'You and I both know now that everyone is precious and the same. Hollywood or homeless, we know that,'" she said, using my dad's exact tone of voice. "There are possibilities beyond your wildest imaginations that will manifest through your trust. *You are heaven,* so wink *to* Heaven now instead of getting winks *from* Heaven—that is your graduation from this course. You are ready for the next one."

Therese laughed. "There's a double meaning with 'course,' both with a meal and with a class you might take. Spirit is so funny," she said, exhaling quickly a few times. "He's showing me a chest of gold coins; that's what enriches you—the experiences. Once you know who you are, you don't *need* the gold coins—you are enough. It's all richness of life. *You are everything you need. Everything you need is within you.*"

I GOT in the car to head home. I turned on my BlackBerry and saw an email from my mom.

> Kathleen Worthington has forwarded you this listing from craigslist.

Oh Jesus.

> Host and Producers wanted for television shows. We are looking for enthusiastic and creative hosts and producers.

I scrolled down to see if there was any money involved.

"This is a paid position," it read at the end.

Hey! We're getting closer!

I quickly responded to the link and then started to drive home. At that moment, my phone rang.

"Hello?" I said.

"Hey, turn on WGN right now," Clay said.

I flipped on my radio and listened to a person who sounded like they'd never been on the air as they stumbled all over their words.

"What is this?" I asked.

"That radio show you didn't get," he said. "It's just *awful*," he laughed. "They've got these writers talking about their blogs with two-word answers. It's such a train wreck. You are so lucky you didn't get this job."

"Hey," I said, feeling sorry for the writer stuttering on the radio. "They're trying their best."

"Yeah, well their best isn't good enough. Okay, I gotta go pick up Britt. Just wanted you to tune in really quick. I'll see you at home."

"Okay, bye," I said, hanging up.

"So, your blog is about how you don't have a car?" I heard the radio host ask his guest.

"Yep," the voice said.

There was an awkward pause that seemed to last for days. I turned off the radio.

Sometimes a huge disappointment winds up being a blessing in disguise.

"Thank you in advance for the job that lets me be myself, express my creativity, and pay my mortgage," I yelled to the sky as I weaved my way through traffic.

When I got home, I looked down and saw an email on my Black-Berry. It was from the folks I had just emailed. They'd looked at my website and wanted to discuss ways we could partner on future projects.

That was fast!

LATER THAT night, Britt and I geared up to watch *A Christmas Story*, or as he called it, "the silly guy movie."

BZZZZZZZZZZZZ.

I heard the BlackBerry vibrate on the coffee table. I walked over and picked it up, and hit the "off" button.

"Scary guy, Mommy!" Britt said, pointing to Scott Farkas as

he tried to beat up Ralphy. I took the remote control and fast-forwarded past the bully scenes and got back on the couch.

"Snuggy with me," Britt said, holding his Binkers.

I looked out the window and watched Clay drape enough lights on our bushes to make Clark Griswold jealous. I held my son tight in my arms and kissed his cute little head as we rocked back and forth.

I was *doing my best* to be Britt's mom. And all was right in the world.

afterword

As I WAS writing this book, I found myself having a wicked case of writer's block when I got to the Millard Fuller portion in San Diego. Part of me was overwhelmed with grief that he had died, that I couldn't call him and reminisce about the conference. Another part was in a panic that I had a deadline I might miss.

I took a walk to get some air and started talking to him.

"Hey, Millard. I don't know if you can hear me. You're probably helping to build some houses for needy kids in Heaven as we speak. But if you are there, and you can inspire me even for a moment, I would be so grateful. You are such an angel. Thank you in advance for even considering this request."

I went back to my office and sat down at the computer. I wrote for the next several hours without coming up for air. My memory of the Millard events was so crystal clear, I could taste the fish I had from dinner all over again.

The next morning, I reread my chapter and smiled with satisfaction. Suddenly, my BlackBerry went off. I looked down and read the subject of my new email.

From the Fuller Center for Housing . . .

Staring me in the eyes was an email from Millard's organization. I had never received one from them before, but now I was the recipient of their newsletter.

That was a good one, Millard!

Whether you call it coincidence or a wink from above, the timing was perfect. I knew that everything else with this book would fall into place. I scrolled down to another email from a name I didn't recognize.

Dear Jen:

I wanted to ask you a question about judgment. I was raised Catholic, and feel guilty about everything. I am a single mom and because of this tough economy, I have had to resort to getting a second job dancing for a strip club. Does that mean I'm going to hell?

I never expected to be a dancer. The father of my son left me and my family doesn't talk to me because I got pregnant before I was married. I was blessed with a nice figure, and someone suggested I dance because the money is good.

Now I put food on the table, but every single day I feel like God is frowning on my choices. I don't drink. I don't do drugs. I don't sleep around. Yet because I happen to walk around in a g-string for a paycheck, I am worried I'll burn in hell.

I know you interviewed a lot of gurus, and to be honest, I don't have the energy to read when I get home. It's kind of amazing that I even read *your* book, but it didn't feel like a book—because I laughed a lot. Anyways, thanks for taking the time to answer this if you can. I really appreciate it.

Signed,
"Dancing in the 'burbs"

I quickly hit "reply" and wrote a response.

Dear "Dancing in the 'burbs,"

I am sorry you have such guilt for your choices. I know from several interviews, not only with gurus but also with Catholic priests, that man judges a lot more than God does. You sound like a dedicated mom with some annoying family members who are lost in a system of punishment and repetition. Wouldn't it be amazing if they took a minute to feel your love, rather than point a finger from the front pew of church? I believe we all do the best we can in every moment. And that God loves you . . . even if you're dangling from a stripper pole.

Keep in touch!
Jen

THANK YOU in advance, Universe, for inspiring those who read this book and helping them remember that we are never alone. And if you really want to raise your vibration or the vibration of those around you, don't bother with the spiritual retreat or three-week cleanse. Just keep a *Flashdance* energy bucket handy, and you should be in pretty good shape.

acknowledgments

TRYING TO thank people for their help on this book is a daunting task . . . Do I do it alphabetically, so nobody gets upset about their placement in the lineup? Maybe I should thank people in the order of how they show up in the story? (Problem is—some people asked me to change their names—so if I'm thanking "James," there is no guy named "James" who will read it and go "wow—how cool that I was thanked in the acknowledgments.") Even worse is I've asked lots of people to give me quotes for the book cover—but we haven't heard back from many of them yet. Do you see my dilemma?

This book would not be possible without Greg Brandenburgh. He believed in my humorous take on spirituality from day one, and then got Amber Guetebier on board—an incredible editor and overall "cool chick." (Big bonus is they gave me reasons to visit San Francisco—which inspired my writings and fed my soul.) All the folks at Red Wheel Weiser and Hampton Roads have been so professional and supportive—especially Tania Seymour, Bonni Hamilton, and Rachel Leach.

Thanks to my literary agent Bill Gladstone for not giving up until he found me a publisher for my first book, *Stay Tuned*. There would have been no second book if Bill hadn't helped me get my first.

I would most likely be cranking out fear-based news stories for a major network and hating every minute of it had I not met Therese Rowley. She uses her gift selflessly, and her wise insights gave me MOST of my material. Caroline Myss, Deepak Chopra, don Miguel Ruiz, Wayne Dyer, Dr. Judith Orloff, Liz Gilbert, and Master John Douglas are the others whose teachings provided experiences that are now chapters in this book.

My media friends Richard Roeper, John St. Augustine, Steve Cochran, Falise Platt, Linda Jack, Rick Kogan, Eric Furguson, Jonathan Brandmeier, Sam Samuelson, and Laura Caldwell all helped me get the word out about my new career path. Your generosity has changed lives.

My husband Clay and son Britt were always there to remind me that I'm unconditionally loved. To Teddi, Rafer, Tiffany, Mom, Martha, and all the Champlins, Weigels, Worthingtons, and Britts who supported my adventures. To the Mencoffs and the Minasians for always treating me like extended family.

Thanks to everyone who shared their stories with me and allowed me to put them in this book.

And for anyone who is struggling to find their way in a world full of judgment and pain: Look for the signs, remember to laugh, and stop punishing yourself.

Because everyone deserves to be spiritual, dammit!

hampton roads
publishing company

. . . for the evolving human spirit

Hampton Roads Publishing Company
publishes books on a variety of subjects,
including spirituality, health, and other
related topics.

For a copy of our latest trade catalog,
call 978-465-0504 or visit our website at *www.hrpub.com*